Cambridge E

MW00628799

Elements in Quantitative and Computational Methods
for the Social Sciences
edited by
R. Michael Alvarez
California Institute of Technology
Nathaniel Beck
New York University

TEXT ANALYSIS IN PYTHON FOR SOCIAL SCIENTISTS

Prediction and Classification

Dirk Hovy
Bocconi University

CAMBRIDGE
UNIVERSITY PRESS

CAMBRIDGE
UNIVERSITY PRESS

University Printing House, Cambridge CB2 8BS, United Kingdom

One Liberty Plaza, 20th Floor, New York, NY 10006, USA

477 Williamstown Road, Port Melbourne, VIC 3207, Australia

314–321, 3rd Floor, Plot 3, Splendor Forum, Jasola District Centre,
New Delhi – 110025, India

103 Penang Road, #05–06/07, Visioncrest Commercial, Singapore 238467

Cambridge University Press is part of the University of Cambridge.

It furthers the University's mission by disseminating knowledge in the pursuit of
education, learning, and research at the highest international levels of excellence.

www.cambridge.org
Information on this title: www.cambridge.org/9781108958509
DOI: 10.1017/9781108960885

First published 2022

A catalogue record for this publication is available from the British Library.

ISBN 978-1-108-95850-9 Paperback
ISSN 2398-4023 (online)
ISSN 2514-3794 (print)

Text Analysis in Python for Social Scientists

Prediction and Classification

Elements in Quantitative and Computational Methods for the Social Sciences

DOI: 10.1017/9781108960885
First published online: February 2022

Dirk Hovy
Bocconi University
Author for correspondence: Dirk Hovy, dirk.hovy@unibocconi.it

Abstract: Text contains a wealth of information about a wide variety of sociocultural constructs. Automated prediction methods can infer these quantities (sentiment analysis is probably the most well-known application). However, there is virtually no limit to the kinds of things we can predict from the text: power, trust, and misogyny are all signaled in language. These algorithms easily scale to corpus sizes infeasible for manual analysis. Prediction algorithms have become steadily more powerful, especially with the advent of neural network methods. However, applying these techniques usually requires profound programming knowledge and machine learning expertise. As a result, many social scientists do not apply them. This Element provides the working social scientist with an overview of the most common methods for text classification, an intuition of their applicability, and Python code to execute them. It covers both the ethical foundations of such work as well as the emerging potential of neural network methods.

Keywords: text analysis, natural language processing, computational linguistics, classification, prediction

JEL classifications: A12, B34, C56, D78, E90

ISBNs: 9781108958509 (PB), 9781108960885 (OC)
ISSNs: 2398-4023 (online), 2514-3794 (print)

Contents

Introduction   1

Background: Classification and Prediction   2

1   Ethics, Fairness, and Bias   3

Prediction: Using Patterns in the Data   11

2   Classification   11

3   Text as Input   17

4   Labels   20

5   Train-Dev-Test   22

6   Performance Metrics   25

7   Comparison and Significance Testing   29

8   Overfitting and Regularization   33

9   Model Selection and Other Classifiers   36

10   Model Bias   40

11   Feature Selection   41

12   Structured Prediction   45

Neural Networks   54

13   Background of Neural Networks   54

14   Neural Architectures and Models   70

References   83

Introduction

Social science has embraced text analysis as a welcome tool in its arsenal. However, in many cases, the analysis has focused on inductive techniques like topic modeling, clustering, or dimensionality reduction, which in machine learning (ML) are called "unsupervised." These techniques are designed to take text as input and find structures that help us explain it. Unsupervised, exploratory methods were the focus of a previous Element in this series (Hovy, 2020).

In this Element, we focus on *predictive* techniques – that is, we assume text captures and expresses an external construct, behavioral variable, or label. This approach to text analysis is rarer in the social sciences than unsupervised induction but is growing. (For an overview in different disciplines, see Chatsiou and Mikhaylov [2020]; Evans et al. [2007]; Humphreys and Wang [2017], inter alia.) We usually have one of two goals: either to gain insights into the terms and phrases that signal the construct of interest or to extend the classification from a small sample to a large corpus of text.

For example, De Choudhury et al. (2013, 2014) have used social media data to predict the occurrence of postpartum depression. Park et al. (2015) showed that personality traits like the Big five can be reliably inferred from Twitter posts. Eliashberg et al. (2007) predicted box office success based on movies' IMDb summaries. Coussement and Van den Poel (2008) forecasted customer churn based on complaints received in customer-support emails. In addition, Gerber (2014) studied the effect of using tweets to forecast the prevalence of various types of crime in Chicago neighborhoods.[1]

In all of these cases, text was used as input to predict the construct or dependent variable of interest. However, predictions based on text can also be used to infer or complete missing values that serve as independent variables in another model. For example, Tirunillai and Tellis (2012) have used the valence of reviews (positive or negative) as one of the input variables used to predict stock market performance.

This Element assumes familiarity with Python, as well as a basic understanding of how to represent text computationally. As a refresher of this last aspect, readers should see Hovy (2020) All the code in this Element can be downloaded from `https://github.com/dirkhovy/text_analysis_for_social_science`.

---

[1] This work raises both methodological questions (topics models should not be used as input for classifiers due to their variability) and ethical concerns (crime forecasting has been shown to reinforce stereotypes and contain a strong bias). We will discuss these aspects in later sections.

BACKGROUND: CLASSIFICATION AND PREDICTION

Imagine you open your email in the morning to find the following message:

> Greetings dear friend
>   We have an amazing offer 4U: Click here to get access to a free con-
> sultation for serious wealth benefits! Urgent: offer expires soon. Works
> guaranteed! Triple your income.

You would probably sigh, mark the message as spam, and move on with your
day. Maybe you would wonder why your spam filter failed to catch this message or how well it does its job in general. Below that message you see an
email from your colleague, telling you that due to a glitch in the experimental setup, the demographic information for yesterday's survey participants was
not recorded. The survey was anonymous, so there is no way to get in touch
with them. Would there be a way to impute the missing values, your colleague wonders? You then turn your attention to another project, for which you
will need to present subjects with text that looks real enough but is not actually copied from any source. Will you have to write all of those examples by
hand?

All of these things are, in fact, topics for this Element. Recognizing a message
as spam based on certain terms is a task we want to automate by building a classifier. In order to do so, we need exactly the kind of data you have produced:
messages labeled as spam. We will see how we can evaluate the performance of
these classifiers and where their blind spots are. Even the problem of the missing values is something classifiers can help us with. We will see how we can
predict various author demographics from the text. Finally, the task of producing real-looking fake text is also a prediction problem: given an empty page,
predict the "best" first word of a sentence. After that, keep predicting more
words, given the context you have created.

Lately, neural networks have gotten incredibly good not only at generating
fake text but also at prediction tasks in general. We will take a look at what
makes these networks special and discuss how to think about the power and
ethical implications of using these tools.

Prediction is useful for inferring both linguistic structure (parts of speech, syntax, named entity recognition, and discourse structure) and a multitude of social
constructs that are signaled in language. The most well-known application of
prediction is probably sentiment analysis, classifying whether a document is
positive, negative, or neutral. However, there is virtually no limit to the kind of
things we can predict from the text: power, trust, misogyny, age, gender, and

so on (Niculae et al., 2015; Peskov et al., 2020; Prabhakaran et al., 2012; Sap et al., 2020, among others).

Prediction is a core part of ML and essentially involves showing the computer lots of examples of inputs (in our case, documents) as well as the correct output labels for them (e.g., *spam* or *no spam*, or *positive, negative*, or *neutral*). Note that we can have any number of possible output labels (**classes**). Since language is one of the most individual human capabilities, it also reveals a lot about the person using it. The predictive models we build can expose people's profiles and characteristics without them being aware of what they revealed.

Because we try to predict the class labels of new input, prediction is synonymous with **classification**. If, instead of classes, we predict a continuous numerical value, we refer to this value as **regression**. In the social sciences, there are some cases where we would like to do regression, but there are practically no use cases in natural language processing (NLP). The principles described in subsequent sections are largely analogous for regression, but we will not cover them in detail.

Prediction is a handy application of ML, for both NLP and the social sciences. It allows us to infer variables of interest (power relations, buying intent, etc.) and complete missing variables (e.g., age and gender) based on language. The principles behind these models are relatively simple. With sufficient data and ever more powerful models, it is easy to get carried away with the possibilities.

We will look at the basic principles behind classification, learn how to set up experiments in a realistic way (see pages 22 and 24) to evaluate the performance (see page 25), test the significance of our performance results (see page 29), and prevent overfitting (see page 33). We will then look at how to improve the predictive performance of the models using a variety of techniques (see page 41).

In Sections 13 and 14 of this Element, we will take a look at neural networks. This is a booming area of research, with a history that dates to the 1950s, so we will only be able to cover the basics (see page 57), as well as a number of model architectures that have shown themselves especially useful for text analysis (see pages 63, 70, 73 and 77).

With great power comes great responsibility, so before we delve deeper into the algorithmic side of prediction, let's look at its ethical aspects.

1 Ethics, Fairness, and Bias

You have a data set with survey answers. For some participants, you have information about their age and gender. However, you ran several trials, and in some of them, you forgot to have subjects provide their demographic information, so now you have missing data. Since controlling for gender would be a handy thing to do for your study, you decide to train a classifier on the subset of the data for which gender information is available and then apply the classifier to the rest of the data. That way, you can impute the missing demographic information. Your classifier performs well, and you complete the study and are now able to control for the effect of gender.

As you look at the data again, though, you realize that it has a bias. Most of the participants who did provide gender information were women, so the classifier is much better at identifying women. It also suggests women more often. You now suspect that the gender distribution on the entire data set is skewed toward predicted female participants. You also realize that you have essentially created a tool that can infer gender where people did not provide it. Maybe they just forgot, or maybe they did not want to reveal this information. Is it OK to still use your tool on the data? Obviously, you are only interested in answering a scientific question, but you realize that someone could use your tool with much less honorable motives.

With great (predictive) power comes great responsibility and especially when working with language, there are a number of ethical questions that arise. There are no hard-and-fast rules for everything, and the topic is still evolving, but several topics have emerged so far. While the overview here is necessarily incomplete, it is a starting point on the issue.[2]

Originally, ML and NLP were about solving fairly artificial problems on small data sets, with the promise of rerunning them on larger data at some later point. While there has always been a certain amount of skepticism and worry about AI's power, until recently, these worries were largely theoretical. In essence, there was not enough data and computational power for these systems to make an impact on people's lives.

As large amounts of data have become available, and with the universal application of ML, we have finally reached a point where AI's theoretical impact has become a reality. With the focus on making useful tools, we have moved away from explanatory and descriptive models (to understand *why* they returned a certain result) to predictive models. These are harder to analyze, but they produce excellent predictions.

It now turns out that one of the reasons why models have gotten so good at prediction is because they pick up on things that they were not meant to exploit. Embedding models reflect ethnic and gender stereotypes (Bolukbasi

---

[2] This chapter is based on the work by Hovy and Spruit (2016), Shah et al. (2020), as well as the ACL workshops on Ethics in NLP.

et al., 2016); bail decision predictions are majorly influenced by the defendants' ethnicity (Angwin et al., 2016); automatic captioning and smart speakers do not work for people with nonstandard language varieties (Harwell, 2018; Tatman, 2017); and skin cancer detectors work only on white skin (Adamson & Smith, 2018).

All of these unintended consequences are examples of **bias**: a systematic difference from the truth. These biases can arise from the data, the models, or the research design itself.

Bias is not necessarily a problem a priori. In the behavioral psychology tradition, biases are mental shortcuts that help us save time and energy. In Bayesian statistics, the prior is a bias: it captures what we expect to encounter before we have any evidence. Expecting someone from Germany to have a German accent in English is a bias, but it means we won't be surprised if they do have an accent and will understand them better. A bias becomes problematic, though, when we trust it more than the data or when we let it govern decisions.

In language data, demographic biases are powerful since we use language to consciously and subconsciously signal who we are. Language therefore reflects a lot of information about our age, gender, ethnicity, region, personality, and even things like our profession and income bracket.

This leads to a second problem with better and better predictive models, namely **privacy**. At this point, we can use NLP systems that exploit the signals in our language used to predict all of the aforementioned features: people's age (Nguyen et al., 2011; Rosenthal & McKeown, 2011), gender (Alowibdi et al., 2013; Ciot et al., 2013; Liu & Ruths, 2013), personality (Park et al., 2015), job title (Preoţiuc-Pietro et al., 2015a), income (Preoţiuc-Pietro et al., 2015b), and much more (Volkova et al., 2014, 2015).

Being able to predict arbitrary demographic and sociocultural attributes puts practitioners in a moral quandary. On the one hand, we want the best tools to answer our questions and make generalizable claims about the world. On the other hand, we do not want to develop tools that could be misappropriated for nefarious goals. This potential for abuse is the third problem, called **dual use**.

1.1 Bias from Data

It is tempting to see bias in ML purely as a data problem, but as we will see throughout the sections of this Element, there are many ways in which bias can creep into our NLP systems. From data alone, there are two ways in which bias can enter into our work: data selection and annotation. Choosing a demographically nonrepresentative data set introduces **selection bias**.

When choosing a text data set with which to work, we are also making deci-sions about the demographic groups represented in the data. As a result of the demographic signals present in language, any data set carries a **demographic bias**, that is, latent information about the demographic groups present in it. As humans, we would not be surprised if someone who grew up hearing only their dialect had trouble understanding other people. So if our data set is dominated by the "dialect" of a specific demographic group, we should not be surprised that our models have problems understanding others.

Most data sets have some kind of built-in bias, and in many cases, it is benign. It becomes problematic when these biases negatively affect certain groups or advantage others. When applied to biased data sets, statistical models will over-fit the presence of specific linguistic signals that are particular to the dominant group. As a result, the model will work less well for other groups, that is, it will lead to the **exclusion** of demographic groups.

Hovy and Søgaard (2015) and Jørgensen et al. (2015) have recently shown the consequences of exclusion for NLP. Parts-of-speech (POS) tagging models are significantly less accurate for young people, as well as ethnic minorities, vis-à-vis the dominant demographics in the training data. Apart from exclusion, these models will pose a problem for future research. Given that a large part of the world's population is currently under thirty,[3] such models will degrade even more over time and ultimately not meet the needs of their users.

This issue also has severe ramifications for the general applicability of any findings using these tools. In psychology, most studies are based on college students, a very specific demographic: western, educated, industrialized, rich, and democratic research participants (so-called WEIRD [Henrich et al., 2010]). The assumption that findings from this group would generalize to all other demographics has proven wrong – and has led to a heavily biased corpus of psychological data and research.

1.1.1 Countermeasures

Potential countermeasures to demographic selection bias can be simple. Post-stratification is the downsampling of overrepresented groups in the training data to even out the distribution until it reflects the actual distribution. Moham-mady and Culotta (2014) have shown how existing demographic statistics can be used as supervision. In general, we can use measures designed to address overfitting or imbalanced data to correct for demographic bias in data. Avoid-ing biased selections is even better, so when creating new data sets, NLP

---

[3] www.socialnomics.net/2010/04/13/over-50-of-the-worlds-population-is-
-under-30-social-media-on-the-rise/

researchers have been encouraged to provide a **data statement** (Bender & Friedman, 2018). This statement includes various aspects of the data collection process and the underlying demographics. It provides future researchers with a way to assess the effect of any bias they might notice when using the data. As a useful side effect, it also forces us to consider the makeup of our data.

1.2 Bias from Research Design

Most NLP research is still on English and in English. It generally focuses on Indo-European data/text sources rather than on small languages from other language groups, for example, in Asia or Africa (Joshi et al., 2020). Even if there is a potential wealth of data available from other languages, most NLP tools skew toward English (Munro, 2013; Schnoebelen, 2013).

This **underexposure** of other languages creates an imbalance in the available amounts of labeled data. It also reproduces itself. Because most of the existing labeled data cover only a few languages, most existing research focuses on those languages. Consequently, this research then creates even more resources for those languages. This dynamic makes new research on smaller languages more difficult, and it naturally directs new researchers toward languages that are already overrepresented. The focus on English may therefore be self-reinforcing. The existence of off-the-shelf tools for English makes it easy to try new ideas in English. Startup costs are much higher to explore other languages in terms of data annotation, basic analysis models, and other resources.

There are little in the way of semantic or syntactic resources for many languages. In a random sample of tweets from 2013, we found thirty-one different languages. There were no treebanks (resources with annotations for syntactic structure) for eleven of them and even fewer semantically annotated resources like WordNets.[4] Consequently, researchers are less likely to work on those languages.

Conversely, the prevalence of resources for English has created **overexposure** to this variety, even though both the morphology and syntax of English are global outliers. The overexposure to English (as well as to certain research areas or methods) creates a bias described by the **availability heuristic** (Tversky & Kahneman, 1973). If we can recall something more easily, we infer that this thing must be more important, bigger, better, more dangerous, and so on. For instance, people estimate the size of cities they recognize to be larger than that of unknown cities (Goldstein & Gigerenzer, 2002). The same holds for languages, methods, and topics we research. Would we have focused on *n*-gram

---

[4] Thanks to Barbara Plank for the analysis!

models to the same extent if English was as morphologically complex as, say, Finnish?

Lately, researchers have used many approaches to develop multi- and cross-lingual NLP tools for linguistic outliers. However, there are simply more commercial incentives to overexpose English rather than other languages. Even though other languages are equally fascinating from a linguistic and cultural point of view, English is one of the most widely spoken languages. It is therefore also the biggest market for NLP tools.

Overexposure can also create or feed into existing biases. If research repeatedly found that the language of a particular demographic group was harder to process, this research could create a situation where this group was perceived to be more difficult, especially in the presence of preexisting biases. The confirmation of biases through the gendered use of language, for example, has been cited as being at the core of second- and third-wave feminism (Mills, 2012). Overexposure thus creates biases that can lead to discrimination. To some extent, the frantic public discussion on the dangers of AI is a result of overexposure (Sunstein, 2004).

There are no easy solutions to this problem, which might only become apparent in hindsight. In their absence, it can help ask ourselves counterfactuals: Would I research this if the data wasn't as easily available? Would my finding still hold for another language? We can also try to assess whether the research direction of a project feeds into existing biases or whether it overexposes certain groups.

1.3 Privacy

In the wake of the Cambridge Analytica scandal, it has become apparent that our data is not as secret and private as we would like to think. To address the problem of unethical data sharing, the European Parliament has enacted a law designed to protect privacy online: the **General Data Protection Regulation** (GDPR).

The GDPR makes some provisions for research purposes (as opposed to commercial purposes). Non-protected categories can still be predicted for research purposes. Even protected categories are OK to use, as long as they cannot be used to identify individual subjects. Still, the law does not give researchers carte blanche to be negligent with subject data. If it becomes necessary to estimate the overall prevalence of gender or sexual orientation in the data, we can use models to infer these in aggregate. It is, however, not OK to use them to profile individual subjects.

1.3.1 Countermeasures

We can help protect our subjects' privacy by keeping data sources separate from each other. To ensure that we can still learn from all of these sources, we can use techniques called **federated learning** (Konečný et al., 2016). Coavoux et al. (2018) have shown that neural network architecture choices can help protect users' privacy. However, there is also cautious evidence that this protection might not be as bulletproof as we might hope (Elazar & Goldberg, 2018).

1.4 Normative versus Descriptive Ethics

Biased models and data sets are a nuisance when used to train a classifier. However, they can also offer a window into the nature of society. This property illustrates an interesting distinction between **normative ethics** and **descriptive ethics**: We use language to express opinions, and because word embeddings capture semantic similarity, they also capture how much writers associate two terms. This association is reflected in the fact that word embeddings show a high similarity between "woman" and "homemaker" and between "man" and "programmer." When biased word embeddings are used as input for predictive models, the inherent bias is clearly negative (Bolukbasi et al., 2016) and therefore normatively wrong for many applications (e.g., for reviewing job candidates, where ideally, we would want all genders or ethnicities to be equally associated with all jobs). However, several social science studies have picked up on the insight provided by the biases contained in word embeddings. Works by Garg et al. (2018) and Kozlowski et al. (2018) have shown that we can use precisely this property to study evolving societal attitudes about gender roles and ethnic stereotypes by measuring the distance between certain sets of words in different decades. Similarly, Bhatia (2017) has shown that this property of word embeddings can be used to measure people's psychological biases and attitudes toward making certain decisions. This bias is therefore descriptively correct.

In contrast, Google Translate used "he" to translate the gender-neutral Turkish pronoun "o" as referring to a doctor but used "she" when referring to a nurse. This translation is both normatively and descriptively wrong (we do not want to assume a world where only men can be doctors, and the back-translated sentence is not the same as the one we started with). While it is normatively wrong that Google Search autocompletes the query "why are Americans" with "so fat," it is also descriptively insightful (because completions are based on people's search queries), at least as far as stereotypes are concerned.

1.5 Dual Use

The ethics philosopher Hans Jonas has cautioned that any technology that is possible will be used for both good and bad (Jonas, 1984). Even if we do not intend any harm in our experiments, the biases they contain can still have unintended consequences that negatively affect people's lives. The most well-known (and extreme) example is physics and the atom bomb. Physicists had to confront the fact that some of their most well-intentioned findings could be (and ultimately were) used to kill.

While in no way as extreme, text analysis techniques can have mixed outcomes as well. On the one hand, they can vastly improve search and educational applications (Tetreault et al., 2015), on the other they can also reenforce prescriptive linguistic norms when they work poorly for nonstandard language. Stylometric analysis can shed light on the provenance of historic texts (Mosteller & Wallace, 1963) and aid forensic analysis of extortion letters, but it can also endanger the anonymity of political dissenters. Text classification approaches can help decode slang and hidden messages (Huang et al., 2013) but have the potential to be used for censorship and suppression. At the same time, NLP can also help uncover such restrictions (Bamman et al., 2012). Hovy (2016) shows that simple NLP techniques can be used not only to detect fake reviews but also to generate them in the first place.

All these examples indicate that we should become more aware of the way other people appropriate NLP technology for their purposes. We also need to be mindful that NLP research is and will be used for unwanted applications. Automated censorship and the measuring of party-line adherence online to punish dissenters are two examples. Statistical models make both of these uses possible. The unprecedented scale and availability of data and models can make the consequences of new technologies hard to gauge.

These examples show that moral considerations go beyond immediate research projects. The role of the researcher in ethical discussions has been pointed out by Rogaway (2015) and the moral obligations of practicing data scientists by O'Neil (2016). As practitioners, we need to be aware of the duality of our work – its ability to be used for both good and bad ends – and openly address it. We may not be held directly responsible for the unintended consequences of our research or products, but we should acknowledge how they can enable morally questionable or sensitive practices; raise awareness in our customers, colleagues, and students; and lead the discourse on ethics and NLP in an informed manner.

PREDICTION: USING PATTERNS IN THE DATA

2 Classification

Very often, we are interested in predicting whether a document belongs to a particular class of interest: Is it an ad or not (**spam filtering**)? Is it positive, negative, or neutral in tone (**sentiment analysis**)? Was it written by an older or a younger person (**author attribute prediction**)? Most of these applications are commercial. Still, predictive approaches based on text are becoming more and more common in the social sciences as well. Suppose we can predict from a speech which party a politician belongs to or whether a report outlines human rights. These predictions tell us something about the level of political polarization (Peterson & Spirling, 2018) and evolving human rights standards in a given context (Greene et al., 2019). To answer questions about a text, we can use predictive statistical models (or **classifiers**) that have been fitted on training texts to maximize the number of correct predictions on held-out data.

Classification is one of the core ML applications to have gained a lot of attention over the last few years. It can seem complicated and mysterious, but all ML is closely related to statistical methods commonly used in social science. One of the most common (and valuable) classification algorithms is **logistic regression**, the same method used to compute the fit between a set of independent variables and a binary dependent variable in the social sciences. The algorithm is the same, but there are two main differences.

The first set of differences is terminological: instead of independent variables, ML talks about **features**; instead of dependent variables, it uses **targets**, whose values are called **classes** or **labels**; the coefficients (or betas) of the algorithm are referred to as **parameters** or **weights**. We will use the ML terminology here, with occasional translations.

In general, we want to represent the data we work with as **vectors** (i.e., lists of numbers) and **matrices** (i.e., lists of vectors). These formats have the advantage that we can apply all kinds of linear algebra techniques to implement our algorithms, which are theoretically well-founded and computationally fast.[5] We represent each example as a vector X_i, and stack them together to form a **data matrix** X.[6] Each feature is one column in the matrix. The labels for all the instances are stored in a vector y. Formally, each training instance is a

---

[5] Most ML, NLP, and AI boil down to a series of linear algebra operations. It would be technically correct to replace all of them with "matrix multiplication" – but that would not make for nearly as exciting headlines.

[6] We will see a bit later in Section 3 how we transform the text into these matrices.

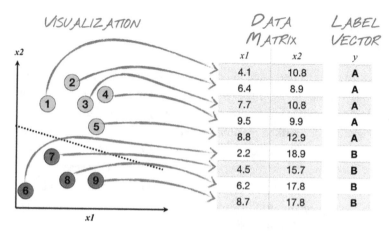

Figure 1 Example of a two-class problem with the data points plotted along their two feature dimensions, colored by class label, and separated by a decision boundary (left), and the corresponding data matrix X with two columns and the label vector y

tuple (X_i, y_i), where X_i is a D-dimensional vector of indicators or real numbers describing the input, and $y \in K$ is the correct output class from a set of possible class labels, K. We also refer to the correct labels as **gold labels** or **ground truth**.

A data point is characterized by the values of all its features. Visually, we can imagine each feature as a dimension in a grid by placing it at a point in space. Ideally, we find dimensions representing the data so that the classes form clusters that are easily separable with a line (or, in more than two dimensions, a hyperplane; see Figure 1 for an example).

Independent of the classifier, we can write all of these approaches as follows:

$$y = f(X; \theta, b)$$

That is, the output value y is a function $f(\cdot)$ of the input X, parametrized by a set of parameters, θ, and a **bias term** b. Depending on the algorithm, θ can be weights, probabilities, or activation functions. We will also see several ways to use b to make our estimates better in Section 8. In the case of a linear model, like logistic regression, $f(X)$ would be

$$\theta \cdot \mathbf{X} + b$$

We multiply each value of X with the corresponding value in θ and sum up the results. We add b and threshold the result to get the output. We can visualize the "matrix view" of this operation as in Figure 2 (we are ignoring b for the moment).

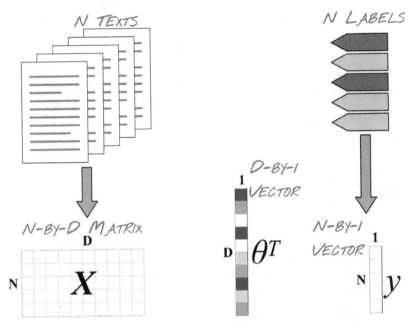

Figure 2 Matrix representation of fitting a classifier: we learn vector θ to transform matrix X into vector y

The output of this binary model is a value between 0 and 1. By checking against a threshold (typically 0.5), we can decide which of the two classes to assign. Once we have fitted our θ vector of weights as in the example afore-mentioned, we can apply it to new data Z (provided it has the same number of columns). The result is our model's predictions. To distinguish the gold labels y from these predictions, we use a hat over the predictions: $\hat{y}$. Mathematically, we can write this as

$$\hat{y} = \theta \cdot \mathbf{Z} + b$$

Graphically, we can represent it as in Figure 3 (again ignoring b for now).

There are many ML classifiers. Logistic regression is the most common, but it can sometimes be good to use support vector machines (SVM; Section 9.1), naive Bayes (Section 9.2), or (feed-forward) neural networks (Section 13). We will cover all of these in later sections. These methods differ only in the ways they weigh and combine the input. However, the principle is always the same: find a pattern of input features, weigh their evidence, and map that to the output target class. You do this yourself when you scan a possible spam email: Does it contain features like "dear friend," "amazing offer," or "FREE"? How likely is each of those to be spam? If it contains only one, it might be ham, but if there are too many red flags, it is probably spam.

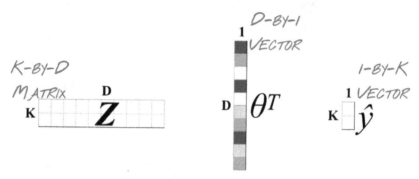

Figure 3 Matrix view of prediction: multiplying a learned weight vector θ with a new data matrix Z to get the prediction vector $\hat{y}$

Suppose we have more than two classes (i.e., a **multi-class** problem), like in sentiment analysis, where we want to choose between three outcomes. In that case, we have two options. We can train a separate binary model for each class (each learns to distinguish instances of that class from all others) and then choose the one with the highest confidence. If we learn a multi-class problem in `sklearn`, the latter is what Python does under the hood. Alternatively, we can train a model that predicts a probability distribution over all the possible output values and then choose the highest ones. This distribution is called a **softmax** (technically, we exponentiate each value before normalizing, which exaggerates initial differences more than "regular" normalization).

The second difference between logistic regression as a classifier in ML and as a regression method in social science is its application: **prediction versus explanation**. In social science, we fit a model to the data to find an explanation. We examine the model coefficients to find an explanatory causal correlation between the independent variables and the dependent variable. Very rarely do we test the predictive power of this model on new data. In ML, in contrast, the objective is only to perform well on new data. After fitting, we freeze the coefficients and measure how well the fitted model predicts new, held-out data. The choice between these two options need not be an either-or: several researchers (Hofman et al., 2017; Shmueli, 2010; Yarkoni & Westfall, 2017) have shown that using ML methods to test the predictive accuracy of a model is a good robustness test. Both fields try to reverse-engineer the underlying data generation process. Ultimately, social science theory is also about predicting how systems (people, markets, and firms) will behave under similar conditions in the future. Every causal model is necessarily also a good predictive model. If we know the causal relation between elements, we can predict how they will develop. The inverse, however, is not necessarily true. A good predictive model might capture aspects that have nothing to do with causality (we will see this when we come to overfitting in Section 8).

2.1 Checklist Text Classification

Here is a step-by-step checklist for how to classify text data and code to implement one possible solution. We will elaborate on the individual steps in the following sections.

(1) Label *at least* 2,000 instances in your data set
(2) Preprocess the text of *all* instances in your data (labeled and unlabeled)
(3) Read in the labeled instances and their labels
(4) Transform the texts into feature vectors using `TfidfVectorizer` or embeddings
(5) Optional: select the top N features (where N is smaller than the number of labeled instances)
(6) Fit a classifier
(7) Use fivefold cross-validation to find the best regularization parameter, top N feature selection, and potentially feature generation and preprocessing steps

```
1  from sklearn.linear_model import LogisticRegression
2  from sklearn.dummy import DummyClassifier
3  from sklearn.feature_extraction.text import TfidfVectorizer
4  from sklearn.model_selection import cross_val_score
5  from sklearn.model_selection import GridSearchCV
6  from sklearn.calibration import CalibratedClassifierCV
7
8  vectorizer = TfidfVectorizer(ngram_range=(1,2),
9                                min_df=0.001,
10                               max_df=0.75,
11                               stop_words='english')
12
13 X = vectorizer.fit_transform(data['clean_text'])
14 y = data['output']
15
16 print(X.shape, y.shape)
17
18 # get baseline performance
19 most_frequent = DummyClassifier(strategy='most_frequent')
20 print(cross_val_score(most_frequent, X, y=y, cv=5, n_jobs=-1,
          scoring="f1_micro").mean())
21
22 # fine-tune classifier
23 base_clf = CalibratedClassifierCV(cv=5,
24     base_estimator=LogisticRegression(n_jobs=-1,
25                                       solver='lbfgs'
26                                       )
27 )
```

```
28 param_grid = {'base_estimator__C': [50, 20, 10, 1.0, 0.5, 0.1,
       0.05, 0.01],
29                'base_estimator__class_weight': ['balanced', 'auto
       ']
30            }
31 search = GridSearchCV(base_clf, param_grid, cv=5, scoring='
       f1_micro')
32 search.fit(X, y)
33
34 # use best classifier to get performance estimate
35 clf = search.best_estimator_.base_estimator
36 print(cross_val_score(clf, X, y=y, cv=5, n_jobs=-1, scoring="
       f1_micro").mean())
```

Code 1 Training a text classifier

```
1 from sklearn.feature_selection import SelectKBest
2 from sklearn.feature_selection import chi2
3 from sklearn.pipeline import Pipeline
4
5 # set up the sequence
6 pipe = Pipeline([
7     ('reduce_dim', 'passthrough'),
8     ('classifier', clf)
9 ])
10
11 # specify selection range
12 N_FEATURES = [1800, 1500, 1000, 500, 300]
13 param_grid = [
14     {
15         'reduce_dim': [SelectKBest(chi2)],
16         'reduce_dim__k': N_FEATURES
17     },
18 ]
19
20 # fit the model to different feature sets
21 grid = GridSearchCV(pipe, n_jobs=1, param_grid=param_grid, cv=5,
       scoring='f1_micro')
22 grid.fit(X, y)
23
24 # save the best selector
25 selector = grid.best_params_['reduce_dim']
26 X_sel = selector.transform(X)
27
28 # refit classifier on entire, dimensionality-reduced data set
29 clf.fit(X_sel, y)
30
31 cv_reg = cross_val_score(clf, X_sel, y=y, cv=5, n_jobs=-1,
       scoring="f1_micro")
32 print("5-CV on train: {}".format(cv_reg.mean()))
```

Code 2 Feature selection

Once you are satisfied with the results and want to apply the classifier to new data:

(1) read in the (unlabeled) new data;
(2) use the `TfidfVectorizer` from above step 5 to transform the new instances into vectors;
(3) use the `SelectKBest` selector from above step 6 to get the top N features;
(4) use the classifier from above step 7 to predict the labels for the new data; and
(5) save the predicted labels or probabilities to your database or an Excel file.

```
1  # read in new data set
2  # transform text into word counts
3  # IMPORTANT: use the same vectorizer we fit on training data to
     create vectors!
4  Z = vectorizer.transform(new_data['clean_text'])
5
6  # select features for new data
7  Z_sel = selector.transform(Z)
8
9  # use best classifier to predict labels
10 predictions = clf.predict(Z_sel)
```

Code 3 Apply classifier to new data

3 Text as Input

Before we can look at the various ways to learn classification problems from text, we need to talk briefly about how to input the text into the computer. Unfortunately, computers still do not process language as we do, so before we can apply any algorithm, we need to transform the text into a computer-readable form: matrices and vectors.

There are two main ways to represent text in vectors: **discrete**, where each position in the vector corresponds to a particular word or phrase, or **distributed**, where the individual positions do not correspond to anything particular. Rather, we have to interpret the vector as a holistic representation of the text in relation to all other texts.

There are many finer points to representing text, which we will not be able to cover here – readers interested in exploring them should see the previous Element (Hovy, 2020). For the purpose of this Element, we can use the following primer.

While texts can come in all kinds of forms and lengths, from short Tweets to entire books, we will generically refer to them as **documents**.

3.1 Discrete Features

The simplest (surprisingly effective) way to translate our texts into a matrix is through something called a **bag-of-words (BOW) model**. We simply go through our data and collect all single words as well as combinations of two and three words (these combinations are also called *n*-grams). This is our **vocabulary**. We discard any term or terms that appear fewer times than a threshold; these terms have no discriminative power. For the same reason, we can discard words that occur too frequently. It is a good idea to make the thresholds percentages of the number of documents in the data, for example, 0.1 percent for the lower threshold and 75 percent for the higher threshold. The remaining terms are our features. We then represent each document as a vector of counts for each of the features. Because not every feature occurs in every document, many of these counts are 0, and we can say that discrete feature vectors are **sparse**.

Rather than using raw occurrence counts (which skew toward longer documents) to determine features, we typically normalize in two ways: by dividing the count for each feature by the total number of features in the document and by the total number of documents in which this feature occurred. The result of the latter operation is called **TFIDF** or term frequency inverse document frequency (Spärck Jones, 1972). The computation is slightly more complex than a simple division, as we have to account for unseen words and outliers. For a more in-depth discussion of the process, see Hovy (2020).

In Python, we can transform a **corpus** (i.e., collection of documents) with the following code. The `min_df` and `max_df` arguments control the word frequency. `sublinear_tf` uses the logarithm of counts to reduce the effect of extremely frequent words.

```
1 from sklearn.feature_extraction.text import TfidfVectorizer
2
3 tfidf_vectorizer = TfidfVectorizer(analyzer='word',
4                                    min_df=0.001,
5                                    max_df=0.75,
6                                    stop_words='english',
7                                    sublinear_tf=True)
8
9 X = tfidf_vectorizer.fit_transform(documents)
```

Code 4 Extracting a TFIDF-weighted discrete representation from a corpus

Discrete representations are interpretable, since each column in our data matrix corresponds to an *n*-gram. However, they are not as good at capturing the meaning similarity between documents as distributed representations.

3.2 Distributed Representations

Distributed representations of features allow us to more fully capture meaning similarity between documents than discrete representations. Instead of collecting a vocabulary and assigning each term to a dimension of the vector representation, distributed representations start by defining a dimensionality, assigning each document a random vector of that dimensionality, and then learning how to best distinguish them.

A more intuitive explanation is to imagine a fridge covered in word magnets. We start by placing words (features) on the fridge at random. Then we begin to organize them based on whether or not they have ever occurred together in the same sentence. Working iteratively, we pick two words and move them closer together if they have occurred together or further apart if they haven't. Eventually, we arrive at some stable constellation. Because of the ordering criterion (occurring in the same sentences), the distances between words now reflect their meaning.

This algorithm is an example of **representation learning** and is called **Word2vec** (Mikolov et al., 2013). It is based on word co-occurrence but can be used to represent documents simply by averaging the vectors of the words in each one. When we extend this approach to entire documents, we call it **Doc2Vec** (originally called `paragraph2vec` [Le & Mikolov, 2014]). Distributed word or document embeddings are called **embeddings**, and because they have to be interpreted holistically, the individual dimensions do not mean anything. However, they are also not sparse, so they need many fewer dimensions to represent the data than vocabulary-based discrete approaches (vocabularies can easily be in the thousands, whereas most embeddings have just dozens or hundreds of dimensions).

In Python, we can use the `gensim` implementation of Word2Vec to learn word embeddings. `sentences` are the input documents; `vector_size` is the number of dimensions we want to use (frequent sizes are 50, 100, 300, or multiples of 8, which are more efficient to compute); `window` is the number of words to either side we want to include when checking whether two words are "in the same sentence"; `min_count` is a frequency threshold; and `workers = -1` parallelizes the process to all cores.

```
1  from gensim.models import Word2Vec
2  from gensim.models.word2vec import FAST_VERSION
3
4  # initialize model
5  w2v_model = Word2Vec(sentences=documents,
6                       vector_size=300,
7                       window=5,
```

```
 8                          min_count=1,
 9                          workers=-1
10 )
11
12 w2v_model.build_vocab(corpus)
13
14 w2v_model.train(corpus, total_examples=w2v_model.corpus_count,
       epochs=w2v_model.epochs)
```

Code 5 Initializing and training a `Word2vec` model

Here, each word is always represented by the same vector, no matter in what sentence it occurs. So the word "bridge" in both "I enjoy playing bridge with my grandparents" and "We can easily bridge that gap" will have the same representation. We will later see how the latest neural language models learn **contextualized embeddings** to address this issue see, Section 14.5.

However, despite this apparent disregard for context, embeddings have also been shown to pick up on social biases in the training data. This can be useful if we wish to study evolving attitudes over time (Bhatia, 2017; Garg et al., 2018; Kozlowski et al., 2018), but it presents an issue when embeddings are used as input for our models. Several papers have shown that these models reproduce and thereby perpetuate biases and stereotypes (Kurita et al., 2019; Tan & Celis, 2019). For example, "woman" is associated with "homemaker" in the same way "man" is associated with "programmer" (Bolukbasi et al., 2016). These societal biases are resistant to many correction methods (Gonen & Goldberg, 2019). When using embeddings, it is therefore good practice to be aware of their biases and check the results for any unwanted stereotypes.

4 Labels

The process of assigning labels to documents is typically called *coding* in the social sciences. However, that term is already reserved for writing code in computational sciences, so the general term used here is **annotations**. This is not the only difference concerning labels between the fields.

In social science, texts are typically annotated by a single person. However, people have quirks and biases. They might be tired and inattentive when they annotate a batch of texts, or they might not be too involved in the task – more focused on the money they will earn for completing it than taking the time to do it well. Annotation decisions made by the individuals who annotate our data introduce **annotation bias**. Sometimes, these biases can arise simply because the annotators are not familiar with the language or style in the data, using their own understanding to label the examples instead of the authors' intended meaning (Sap et al., 2019).

Even with the best intentions, people make mistakes and are inconsistent. In NLP, documents are typically annotated by multiple people, often on crowdsourcing platforms. That redundant annotation allows us to aggregate the answers and find a more robust, unbiased label. It also allows us to determine (1) how reliable annotators are, (2) how difficult specific texts were to label, and (3) how much disagreement exists between annotators. NLP papers will typically report the **inter-annotator agreement** and how the authors aggregated the results. Because multiple annotations are more expensive, papers sometimes measure agreement on only a subset of the data. While theoretically cheaper but equivalent to trained annotators in quality (Snow et al., 2008), it is not always clear whether the demographic makeup of these anonymous workers is representative (Pavlick et al., 2014). Crowdsourcing also raises ethical questions about worker payment and fairness (Fort et al., 2011).

To prevent the effect of annotation bias, we can use **annotation models** (Hovy et al., 2013; Passonneau & Carpenter, 2014; Paun et al., 2018), that is, Bayesian models that infer the most likely answer and the reliability of each annotator. These models help us find biased annotators and let us account for the human disagreement between labels. Implementations of such models are available as software (`https://github.com/dirkhovy/mace`) or web service (`https://mace.unibocconi.it/`). We can even use this quantity in our models' update process (Plank et al., 2014).

Since we are working with matrices and linear algebra operations, we cannot use the actual class names (e.g., "informative," "emotional," "unrelated," etc.) of our output labels internally. `Sklearn` will translate all our text labels into numbers to allow us to do linear algebra. If, however, we want to do this ourselves, `sklearn` lets us translate any collection of labels into numbers starting from 0 using the `LabelEncoder`:

```
1  from sklearn.preprocessing import LabelEncoder
2
3  # transform labels into numbers
4  labels2numbers = LabelEncoder()
5  y = labels2numbers.fit_transform(labels)
```

Code 6 Translating labels into numbers

If we use this numerical representation (again, we do not have to), the classifier output in `sklearn` will also be numbers. Since this is harder to interpret, we have to translate the resulting numbers back into class labels:

```
1 # translate numbers back into original labels
2 predicted_labels = labels2numbers.inverse_transform(predictions)
```

Code 7 Translating predictions back

5 Train-Dev-Test

When we see a new message in our inbox, we usually know pretty quickly whether or not it is spam. There are indicators in the text that help us figure this out based on our experience with previous spam messages. Classifiers work very similarly.

We assume that the output label is related to the input via some function that we need to find by fitting several parameters. This process is called **training**, and it corresponds to our experience with previous spam messages. The training goal is to let the machine find repeated patterns in the data that can be used to estimate the correct output for a new, held-out input example. This new sample is called the **test set**, and in our spam example, it corresponds to a new message in our inbox. We are interested in achieving the highest possible score of some appropriate **performance** metric on the held-out test data.

```
1 from sklearn.linear_model import LogisticRegression
2
3 classifier = LogisticRegression()
4
5 classifier.fit(X, y)
6
7 predictions = classifier.predict(Z)
```

Code 8 Example of fitting a simple logistic regression classifier and applying it to new data to predict its output

Later, we will see how to improve on this basic classifier (Sections 8 and 9). To do that, however, we first need to discuss how to measure these improvements in terms of both data handling and metrics.

We have already briefly discussed the role of the held-out sample for prediction, that is, the test data on which we measure our classifier's performance. But where does that test data come from? If we simply take a new unlabeled text, how can we measure the predictive performance? If we don't know the correct labels for those new data points, what do we compare the predictions against? To simulate encountering new, unseen instances, we divide our data set of (X_i, y_i) pairs into three parts before fitting our model.

The first and largest part of these three subsets is the **training set**, which we will use to fit our model. We also set aside some of the data that we will use as our **test set** and do not use or look at it until we are content with our model. We pretend this data set does not exist. Therefore, we cannot use it to collect words for our vocabulary, look at the distribution of labels, or collect any other statistics.

There is one problem with this setup, though. We usually set several parameters for models, and we will need to find the setting that works best for our particular data sample. To know whether a specific parameter setting works, we need to evaluate it on held-out data. If we adjust the parameters often enough and measure performance on the test data after every time, we will end up with excellent performance. But we will essentially have cheated: we chose the parameters that made it happen! In real life, we could not know these parameters. We can only measure performance on the test set once!

So how *do* we measure the effect a parameter change has on predictive performance if we cannot use the test set? Instead of the test set, we can use another data set, which hopefully approximates the test set. We can use this third data set to see how changing the model parameters affects performance on *a* held-out data set. This second held-out data set, which we use to tune our model parameters, is called the **development set** (or dev set for short).

You can think about this as similar to preparing for an important presentation to funders. You can only present to them once (i.e., they are your test set), but you might want to tweak a few things in the presentation you've prepared (those are your parameters). Since you cannot do a mock presentation with the funders, you ask some colleagues and friends to act as stand-ins. They are your development set. Obviously, the more similar your practice audience is to the funders, the better you will be able to gauge whether you are on the right track.

For the same reason, we want our development and test sets to be as similar to each other as possible, that is, equal size, representative distributions over the outcomes, and large enough to compute robust statistics. To fulfill these conditions, both sets need to be large enough. If we only have ten documents in our dev set, our results will not be representative. It is hard to put a fixed number on the ideal set size, but at the very least, we should have several hundred instances for both of these data sets.

At the same time, we want our training set to be large enough to fit the model correctly. If we have too few documents, we might never see enough combinations to set all the model parameters properly. Again, as a rough guideline, we should have thousands of instances. For a binary classification problem, 1,500 to 2,000 instances are a good start, but more is always better. We will see several ways to improve performance later (Sections 8 and 9). However, the best way is to add more training data. Common ratios of training:development:test

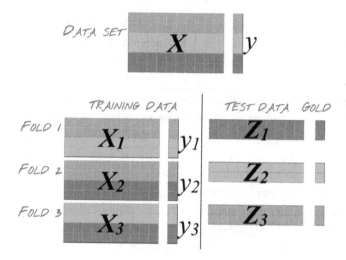

Figure 4 Schematic of threefold cross-validation

data size are 80:10:10, 70:15:15, or 60:20:20, depending on which ratio best satisfies the aforementioned conditions.

5.1 Cross-Validation

This is all well and good, you might say, but I only have a data set of 1,500 documents. If I set aside some of them as a test set I use only once, I will reduce the amount of data I have too much to fit it properly. You have a good point.

If the original data set is too small to allow a large enough test set to be set aside without compromising the fitting process, we can use k-**fold cross-validation**. In k-fold cross-validation, we simulate new data by dividing the data into k subsets, fitting the k model on $k-1$ subsets of the data, and evaluating on the kth subset. See Figure 4 for an example illustration with three folds. Each document has to end up in the held-out part once. In the end, we have performance scores from k models. The average over these scores tells us how well the model will work on new data.

This approach has several advantages: we can measure the performance of the entire data set, simulate different conditions, and get a much more robust estimate. Again, choosing k depends on the resulting training size and the test portions for each fold. k should be small enough to guarantee a decent-sized test set in each fold but large enough to make the training part sufficient. Common values for k are 3, 5, and 10. In the extreme, if $k = N$, the size of our data set, we can fit one model and test it separately for each document in our corpus. This version is also called **leave-one-out cross-validation**.

If we want to have a dev set to tune each of the k models, we can further split each of the $k - 1$ parts of each fold's training portion. In that case, we would train on $k - 2$ parts and tune and test on k parts each.

In Python, we can get stratified subsets of the data (meaning that the label distribution is the same in each set).

```
1 from sklearn.model_selection import StratifiedKFold
2
3 skf = StratifiedKFold(n_splits=3)
4 for train_ids, test_ids in skf.split(X, y):
5     fold_X_train = X[train_ids]
6     fold_y_train = y[train_ids]
7
8     fold_X_test = X[test_ids]
9     fold_y_test = y[test_ids]
```

Code 9 Example of stratified cross-validation

6 Performance Metrics

How good is your spam filter? If a spam email gets through, you might say, "Not great." But one uncaught email, however annoying, doesn't tell you anything about how well the filter is working. How many does it catch? Clearly, we need to be able to measure these things somehow. If someone handed you a classifier and said it was 70 percent accurate, would you use it? What about 80 percent accurate? 90 percent?

In explanatory models, we are usually only interested in the fit of the model to the data. That quantity is typically the r^2 score. While r^2 is *a* performance metric, it is difficult to generalize it to held-out data: How well does a line fit points that we do not yet know? In prediction, we are less interested in the fit than in how well the classifier will predict future cases. We want to measure for how many of the documents in our test data a model produces the correct answer. Depending on how many classes we have and how balanced our data set is for the distribution of these classes, there are different measures we can use. For all of them, we will use the four basic counts: **true positives** (TP; the model prediction and the actual label are the same), **false positives** (FP; the model predicts an instance to be of a specific class, but it is not), **true negatives** (TN; the model correctly recognizes an instance *not* to be of a specific class), and **false negatives** (FN; the model fails to recognize that an instance belongs to a specific class).

Measures of fit and performance metrics need not be mutually exclusive. Yarkoni & Westfall (2017) argued that performance measures can and should be used as an additional measure of robustness. They can also stand in as proxies for other values. Peterson & Spirling (2018) have shown that a higher predictive accuracy of party affiliation correlates with periods of higher polarization. The more polarized their speeches, the easier it is to tell politicians apart.

The most straightforward measure of this performance is **accuracy**, which we determine by simply dividing the number of true positives by the total number of instances, N.

$$acc = \frac{TP + TN}{N}$$

Accuracy is a helpful measure, but it is somewhat less helpful when our labels are unbalanced: in a data set where 90 percent of all labels are class A and 5 percent are classes B and C, a system that always predicts A would get an accuracy of 0.9. (All performance measures are usually given as floating-point values between 0 and 1. However, people may also report accuracy as a percentage.)

When our label distribution is more skewed, we need different measures than accuracy. **Precision** measures how many of our model's predictions were correct. We find it by dividing the number of true positives by the number of all positives.

$$prec = \frac{TP}{TP + FP}$$

If we have only two equally frequent classes, precision is the same as accuracy.

Recall measures how many of the positive examples in the data our model managed to find. We divide the number of true positives by the sum of true positives (the instances our model got right) and false negatives (the instances our model *should* have gotten right but did not).

$$rec = \frac{TP}{TP + FN}$$

A model that classified everything as, say, spam would get a perfect recall for that class. It did, after all, find *all* true positives while not producing any false negatives. However, such a model would obviously be useless since its precision would be terrible.

To get a single number to detect the case aforementioned, we want to balance precision and recall against each other. The **F1 score** does precisely that by taking the harmonic mean between precision and recall.

Table 1 Example output of a classifier and its valuation for different target classes

X	y	ŷ	If target = 1	If target = 0
frog	1	1	TP	TN
deer	1	1	TP	TN
wolf	1	1	TP	TN
dog	1	1	TP	TN
bear	1	1	TP	TN
fish	1	1	TP	TN
bird	1	0	FN	FP
cat	1	0	FN	FP
stone	0	1	FP	FN
tree	0	0	TN	TP

$$F_1 = 2 \times \frac{prec \times rec}{prec + rec}$$

Let's look at a number of examples (see Table 1). We will use the following data from a hypothetical classifier that identifies animals (1) and natural objects (0).

If we are interested in animals, our target label is 1, and we get the following metrics from the measures in the fourth column:

$$acc = \frac{7}{10} = 0.7$$

$$prec = \frac{6}{7} = 0.86$$

$$rec = \frac{6}{8} = 0.75$$

$$F_1 = 0.81$$

If instead our target label is 0 (natural objects), we get the following metrics:

$$acc = \frac{7}{10} = 0.7$$

$$prec = \frac{1}{3} = 0.33$$

$$rec = \frac{1}{2} = 0.5$$

$$F_1 = 0.4$$

Note that accuracy is not affected by how many classes we have or what class we focus on: we only check how often the prediction and the gold data match.

The classes of the matching instances do not matter. For precision, recall, and F1, on the other hand, we need to calculate the score for each class separately. If we have *positive, negative,* and *neutral* as labels, and our target class is *positive,* either of the others is a false negative.

Even if we have several classes and compute precision, recall, and F1 separately, we might still want to have an overall metric. There are two ways of doing this: **micro-** and **macro-averaging**.

In micro-averaging, we add up the raw counts of the positives and negatives. This gives us an average that is weighted by the class size, as larger classes have a greater influence on the outcome.

$$acc_{micro} = 7/10 + 7/10 = 14/20 = 0.7$$
$$prec_{micro} = 6/7 + 1/3 = 7/10 = 0.7$$
$$rec_{micro} = 6/8 + 1/2 = 7/10 = 0.7$$
$$F_{1micro} = 0.7$$

In macro-averaging, we first compute the individual scores for each class and then take the average over them. This gives us an average that weights all classes equally.

$$acc_{macro} = (0.7 + 0.7)/2 = 0.7$$
$$prec_{macro} = (0.86 + 0.33)/2 = 0.6$$
$$rec_{macro} = (0.5 + 0.75)/2 = 0.63$$
$$F_{1macro} = 0.61$$

Which averaging we should use very much depends on the goal we have and how much importance we attach to small classes. There are good reasons to use either scheme.

In Python, we can get all of these performance measures by comparing our classifier's predictions against the gold labels of the held-out data:

```
1 from sklearn.metrics import f1_score, precision_score,
     recall_score
2
3 prec = precision_score(gold, prediction, average="micro")
4 rec = recall_score(gold, prediction, average="micro")
5 f1 = f1_score(gold, prediction, average="micro")
```

Code 10 Examples of evaluation metrics

If we do not have a dedicated held-out set, we can get the average score through cross-validation:

```
1 from sklearn.model_selection import cross_val_score
2
3 prec_cv = cross_val_score(clf, X, y=y, cv=5, n_jobs=-1, scoring=
     "precision_micro")
4 rec_cv = cross_val_score(clf, X, y=y, cv=5, n_jobs=-1, scoring="
     recall_micro")
5 f1_cv = cross_val_score(clf, X, y=y, cv=5, n_jobs=-1, scoring="
     f1_micro")
```

Code 11 Example of micro-averaged evaluation metrics in cross-validation

Instead of micro-averaging, we can use macro-averaging by changing the scoring parameter to M_macro, where M is any of the above metrics. For a full list of all the available cross-validation scoring functions, you can use Code 12:

```
1 import sklearn.metrics as mx
2 sorted(mx.SCORERS.keys())
```

Code 12 Available evaluation metrics for cross-validation

7 Comparison and Significance Testing

When we train a classifier, we want to use it in the future on unseen data. We have seen how we can measure and predict that performance and guard against overfitting. However, while performance measures give us a good sense of the model's capabilities, they do not tell us anything about the classification task's difficulty. Imagine a colleague tells you about their classifier that got an F1 score of 0.9 in distinguishing advice from non-advice in a set of social media posts. It turns out, though, that less than 1 percent of the observations are advice. So what did the classifier learn? Is it really finding those 1 percent of advice cases, or has it "given up" and just classified everything as non-advice? If the data is extremely imbalanced (where most examples are from the same class), even a 0.9 F1 score does not mean much.

To get a sense of the possible headroom, researchers often begin by running a very simple **baseline**. This baseline can be an "algorithm" that always predicts the most frequent class label (**majority baseline**) or another simple model. With nonlinear models (Section 13), we will see that it makes sense to compare against a linear model's baseline. A model that does not even outperform the baseline is probably not on the right track. After all, it does not make sense to use a more complicated model where a simple one suffices.

Sklearn provides a simple implementation of the most frequent label classifier. Since the classifier always returns the most frequent label for everything, we do not even have to use cross-validation. Instead, we can look at the performance of the entire data.

```
1 from sklearn.dummy import DummyClassifier
2 from sklearn.metrics import f1_score
3
4 most_frequent = DummyClassifier(strategy='most_frequent')
5 most_frequent.fit(X, y)
6 most_frequent_predictions = most_frequent.predict(X)
7 print(f1_score(y, most_frequent_predictions, average='micro'))
```

Code 13 Running a baseline classifier that predicts the most frequent label

What if our model outperforms the baseline by some margin? Does that mean another person will see the same results when running the model on their data? Are the improvements over the baseline that we reported a fluke, or do they generalize? This question is at the heart of **statistical significance** tests.[7]

There are several statistical significance tests out there. However, it requires some knowledge to pick the right one for the task at hand (Berg-Kirkpatrick et al., 2012). For many NLP problems, bootstrap sampling is a valid and interpretable test. The intuition behind it is simple: When we compare the results of our model against a baseline, we only have one comparison, which might be biased. The result could very well be due to the particular composition of the data and disappear on a different data set. The best way to address this concern is to test on more data sets. However, if we do not have other samples, we can approximate the effect by simulation. We create different data sets by repeatedly sampling from the data with replacement (**bootstrapping**). We compare both baseline and model performance on each of those samples and record how often that difference is more extreme than on the complete data. The **central limit theorem** says that repeated measures taken from a population follow a normal distribution. Think of a stadium full of people, from which you repeatedly draw five and measure their average height. Most of the time, you will get an average height, and only rarely will you get all the tall people. The average heights will follow a normal distribution. We can use this insight to identify samples where the difference between baseline and model is different from the base case. There are two ways to measure this. The first is the number of samples where the difference deviates more than two standard deviations from the

---

[7] There are also some additional factors to consider: models are sensitive to domain differences – a model trained on newswire will not work well on Twitter data. But say our user wants to apply the model to the same domain.

Table 2 Example performance of two systems on the entire data set (base) and on ten samples

	A	B	Difference
Base	82.13	81.89	0.24
1	81.96	82.03	−0.07
2	81.86	82.61	−0.75
3	81.70	81.44	0.26
4	82.42	82.77	−0.35
5	81.89	81.06	0.83
6	81.39	81.24	0.15
7	81.96	81.58	0.37
8	82.57	81.65	0.92
9	82.50	82.67	−0.17
10	83.07	81.84	1.23

original difference between the systems. The other way is to count negative differences (meaning samples where the better system on the base case is actually worse). The latter case might seem more intuitive, but it requires some assumptions: (1) the mean sample difference is the same as the difference on the entire data set and (2) the distribution over differences is symmetrical. Under those conditions, it is equivalent to the first version. Most NLP measures will fulfill these conditions.

Take the examples in Table 2. On the entire sample, system A is 0.24 points better than system B. If we take enough samples computing the difference between A and B, these differences will follow a normal distribution, and the average difference will be very close to 0.24. With bootstrap sampling, we are asking: *In how many of these samples is the difference at least twice as extreme as in the base case?* This setup requires us to start by putting the system with a higher score on the entire data set. We collect ten samples here (this is only for demonstration purposes; we usually would gather at least 10,000).

Figure 5 shows the distribution over the observed differences. As expected, their average difference is about 0.24, the same as the difference between the systems on the entire data. However, in three cases (samples 5, 8, and 10), the difference is more than twice the base difference. Because the sampled differences follow a normal distribution and because the mean difference is small, there are some cases where A is actually worse than B. These cases indicate that the observed difference is not significant. The *p*-value here would be $3/10 = 0.3$. (Again, in a real test, we would use a much higher number of

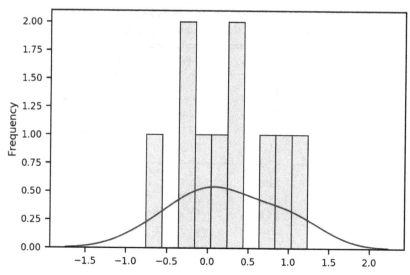

Figure 5 Distribution over differences between the two systems on ten samples

samples, which would make the result more exact and more reliable.) As the base difference increases, there are fewer and fewer extreme cases.

```
1  import numpy as np
2
3  def bootstrap_sample(system1, system2, gold, samples=10000,
       score=precision_score):
4      """
5      compute the proportion of times the performance difference
       of the
6      two systems on a subsample is significantly different from
       the
7      performance on the entire sample
8      """
9      N = len(gold) # number of instances
10
11     # make sure the two systems have the same number of samples
12     assert len(system1) == N and len(system2) == N, 'samples
       have different lengths'
13
14     # compute performance score on entire sample
15     base_score1 = score(gold, system1, average='binary')
16     base_score2 = score(gold, system2, average='binary')
17
18     # compute the difference
19     basedelta = base_score1 - base_score2
20     assert basedelta > 0, 'Wrong system first, system1 needs to
       be better!'
21
```

```
22    system1 = np.array(system1)
23    system2 = np.array(system2)
24    gold = np.array(gold)
25
26    p = 0
27    for i in range(samples):
28        # select a subsample, with replacement
29        sample = np.random.choice(N, size=N, replace=True)
30
31    # collect data corresponding to subsample
32        sample1 = system1[sample]
33        sample2 = system2[sample]
34        gold_sample = gold[sample]
35
36    # compute scores on subsample
37        sample_score1 = score(gold_sample, sample1, average='
      binary')
38        sample_score2 = score(gold_sample, sample2, average='
      binary')
39        sample_delta = sample_score1 - sample_score2
40
41        # check whether the observed sample difference is at
      least
42        # twice as large as the base difference
43        if sample_delta > 2*basedelta:
44            p += 1
45
46    return p/samples
```

Code 14 Bootstrap sampling for statistical significance tests

8 Overfitting and Regularization

Imagine a (slightly contrived) case where, for some reason, most positive training examples in a text classification task contained the word "Tuesday." This means the presence of "Tuesday" is an excellent feature to predict positive instances from the classifier's perspective. But suppose the new instances we encounter in our test set never contain the word "Tuesday." In that case, the model comes up empty-handed when it tries to classify them. It has been **overfitting** the training data. This issue is similar to memorizing versus understanding. If we memorize that $2 + 2 = 4$, we might be surprised when we are told that $3 + 1$ is also 4. If, instead, we understand how addition works, we will be much less surprised by future cases.

Training (i.e., fitting) a model on too many features can cause the model to memorize parts of the training data. While that is excellent for predicting *those* outcomes correctly, it is entirely useless when encountering new examples.

In most social science scenarios, we only use a small number of independent variables. In ML, we often use thousands of them. When working with text, one of the easiest ways to **featurize** the input is to make each observed word type a feature. Depending on the estimate, English has between 100,000 and 500,000 words, so the number of features quickly becomes enormous. This number of independent variables is frowned upon in the social sciences – and for a good reason.

In the extreme case, if we had more independent variables than observations, we could simply find one variable that explained the data. However, it would be hard to know whether this explanation was valid. In ML, this situation is also frowned upon but for different reasons.

In prediction, we would like to prevent the model from perfectly memorizing the training data. If it does, it will not be able to predict new instances accurately. (Remember the example of $2 + 2 = 4$ and $3 + 1 = 4$). This is where the bias term b we mentioned earlier comes back into it. Choosing a bias that prevents the model from overfitting is called **regularization**. It is always a good idea to regularize our models, even if we do not want to use them for prediction.

We can think of regularization as a way to make memorizing the data harder. As a result, the model will be more prepared to handle different scenarios in the future. It is a bit like athletes who introduce obstacles to their training, swimming with a buoy in tow, for example, or carrying extra weight: by making training harder, we are better prepared for the real thing.

The simplest way to use a bias term is to add some random noise to the data. Because the error is random, the model can never fit it perfectly, so we help avoid overfitting. In social science, the bias term is often called an "**error term**" since we assume some measurement is associated with our inputs.

However, randomness is hard for computers, so we often use normally (in the sense of Gaussian) distributed noise, which in itself is regular. It is already a strong assumption that the noise we encounter is normally distributed. In language, the error distribution might actually follow a power-law distribution.

Instead of guessing at the error distribution, we can tie the bias term to the distribution of our parameters. Ideally, we would like a model that considers all features, rather than putting all its eggs in one basket (as in the "Tuesday" example mentioned previously).

Essentially, such a model would distribute the weights for each feature relatively evenly. We can measure this by looking at the **L2 norm** of the weight vector Θ the root of the sum of squares of all weights. The more evenly distributed the weights are, the smaller this term becomes. The effect is that the model is forced to "hedge its bets" by considering *all* features, rather than putting all its faith in a few of them. It is, therefore, better equipped to deal with

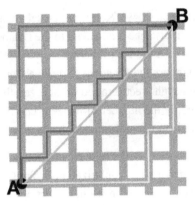

Figure 6 Examples of L1 versus L2 norm in Euclidean space (modified from Wikipedia)

future cases. This process is called **L2 regularization**. The regularization term is usually weighted by a constant called λ.

$$y = \Theta \cdot X + \lambda ||\Theta||_2$$

The L2 norm uses the root of the sum of squares as an error term. Taking the square removes any signs on the elements:

$$||\Theta||_2 = \sqrt{\sum_{i=1}^{N} \theta_i^2}$$

The L2 norm has unique analytical solutions, but it produces non-sparse coefficients (every element has a nonzero value). Therefore, it does not perform variable selection. When we use L2 as regularization for logistic regression, it is also known as **ridge regression**.

Theoretically, we can also minimize the L1 norm of the vector (**L1 regularization**). Here, we use the regular norm of the coefficient vector as the error term:

$$||\Theta||_1 = \sum_{i=1}^{N} |\theta_i|$$

The L1 norm produces sparse coefficients, that is, it sets many coefficients to 0 and therefore has many possible solutions for a given vector. Due to the vectors' sparsity, they all amount to an implicit variable selection: we can ignore all entries with a value of 0 and focus on the others. Using L1 regularization for logistic regression is also known as **lasso regression**.

To see the difference between the two norms, see Figure 6: the red, blue, and yellow lines are all possible L1 solutions with the same value (12), whereas the green line is the L2 solution (8.49). Norms are closely related to distance measures like the Manhattan distance (equivalent to the L1 norm) or the Euclidean distance (which is equivalent to the L2 norm).

More rarely, we might use the **L0 norm** for regularization, which is the sum of all elements in the weight vector raised to their zeroth power (i.e., either 0 or 1) That norm is simply the number of nonzero coefficients. This is a very aggressive way of eliminating uninformative features.

In practice, L2 regularization works best for prediction. In `sklearn`, logistic regression is already set to use L2 regularization, with a C parameter that stands for the λ weight. L1 is most useful in feature selection (Section 7). If we want to use L1, we have to explicitly select it via the `penalty` keyword.

```
1 lasso = LogisticRegression(penalty='l1')
```

Code 15 Defining a logistic regression classifier with L1 regularization (lasso)

9 Model Selection and Other Classifiers

There are, of course, plenty of other classifiers that are not logistic regression, and `sklearn` provides many of them. Thankfully, they all follow the same logic, so we can use the same `fit()` and `predict()` functions from before. In practice, we only need to change one line: where we define the classifier.

Note that each model has a specific set of parameters that govern its behavior (as the regularization parameter for logistic regression). To get the best classifier, we need to tune those parameters. This step is called **model selection**. A model is just one particular combination of parameters. To get the best possible result on our held-out data, we select the highest-performing combination (model).

We can simply iterate over a set of possible values and record which one results in the highest performance.

```
1 from sklearn.metrics import cross_val_score
2
3 best_c = None
4 best_f1_score = 0.0
5
6 for c in [50, 20, 10, 1.0, 0.5, 0.1, 0.05, 0.01]:
7     clf = LogisticRegression(C=c, n_jobs=-1)
8     cv_reg = cross_val_score(clf, X, y=y, cv=5, n_jobs=-1,
        scoring="f1_micro").mean()
9
10    print("5-CV on train at C={}: {}".format(c, cv_reg.mean()))
11    print()
```

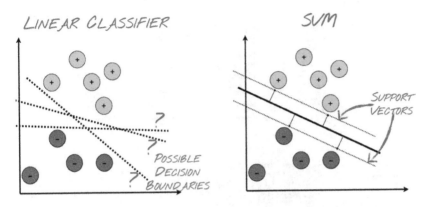

Figure 7 Comparison of a regular linear classifier and an SVM

```
12
13      if cv_reg > best_f1_score:
14          best_f1_score = cv_reg
15          best_c = c
16
17  print("best C parameter: {}".format(best_c))
```

Code 16 Finding the best regularization parameter for logistic regression

If you have few data points (less than 2,000), trying a SVM can help. If you have a lot of data points, naive Bayes can be an option.

9.1 Support Vector Machines

A popular classifier is the SVM. SVMs use a **kernel function** to project the data into a higher-dimensional space and take the similarities between instances in that space into account, which accounts for much of their predictive power. They also try to find the decision boundary between classes that gives the most "room" between them. It does this by computing **support vectors**, that is, vectors parallel to the decision boundary (see Figure 7).

SVMs, therefore, often perform better than logistic regression on small-to medium-sized data sets. However, they become too slow for more massive data sets. Performance crucially depends on the chosen kernel, which also requires the optimization of various parameters. In essence, a kernel function implements a simple way to compute the similarity between two examples in a higher-dimensional space. More dimensions make it easier to find a **hyperplane** that separates classes clearly, even if they were not separable in the original feature space. Some issues remain, though, as we can see in Figure 8.

In `sklearn`, SVM is implemented as `SVC` (the C stands for *classification*).

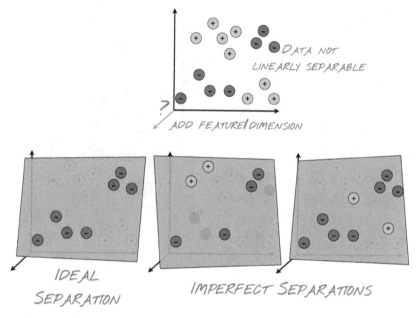

Figure 8 Example of better class separation by adding more dimensions

```
1 from sklearn.svm import SVC
2 svm = SVC()
```

Code 17 The SVM classifier in `sklearn`

The **time complexity** of an algorithm (e.g., how many operations we need to fit a model to the data) depends on the input. Specifically, it depends on the number of observations and features needed to train a classifier. For logistic regression, both are roughly linear, so if we double the number of observations and features, it will take twice as long to fit the data. For an SVM, these numbers are cubic for observations and quadratic for features; the algorithm will take exponentially longer to fit if we double them. This increase is due to the objective function of the SVM, which involves both computing a kernel matrix (i.e., the similarity of all instances with each other) and solving a quadratic function.

The difference between these two tools is mainly due to two facts: (1) SVMs cannot be parallelized, while logistic regression can be and (2) the SVM has a more complex objective function than logistic regression – rather than finding *a* decision boundary, the SVM tries to find the decision boundary that maximizes the distance between classes (the **support vectors** that give the classifier its name), while allowing for some **slack** (i.e., observations being on the wrong side of the decision boundary). These two facts are related: the first is due, in part, to the second.

For details on the time complexity of classification algorithms, see Mohri et al. (2018).

9.2 Naive Bayes

The naive Bayes (NB) algorithm is a very simple generative model. The generative story (i.e., how the observed feature vector was generated) behind NB is simple: We pick a class according to some distribution $P(\mathbf{y})$. Based on that label, we then produce each of the observed feature values with some probability $P(\mathbf{X}|y)$. The features are independent of one another, that is, feature 2 is not influenced by feature 1 or 3 (or any other, for that matter), only by the label. This assumption is, of course, somewhat simplistic (hence the name *naive* Bayes), especially when our features are words in a sentence. Words tend to occur together following specific patterns, not independently of each other. In practice, though, NB works reasonably well, and it has four advantages: (1) it is easy to implement, (2) it is very straightforward to interpret the model, (3) it scales really well to enormous amounts of data, and (4) it parallelizes well (because of its ability to scale).

To find the distribution over class labels $P(y)$, all we have to do is go through our instances, count how often we see each label, and normalize by the total number of instances. Similarly, to find the conditional probability distribution $P(X|y)$ of features given a class, we count how often each feature occurs with each class and divide that by the number of times we have seen that class. To label a new instance, we simply sum all our conditional probabilities from the present features, compute all class probabilities, and then pick the highest one as a label. Or, mathematically:

$$\hat{y} = \arg\max_{y_i \in \mathbf{y}} P(y_i) \prod_{j=1}^{N} P(x_j|y_i)$$

Here, arg max just means, "Pick the value that gives you the highest result for the following equation."

In `sklearn`, NB is implemented in various forms, but the one we would use with discrete features is multinomial NB:

```
1 from sklearn.naive_bayes import MultinomialNB
2 nb = MultinomialNB()
```

Code 18 NB in `sklearn`

NB can also be made to incorporate unlabeled data. If we have no label, we need to compute how often we would see each class *hypothetically*. This quantity is called **fractional or expected counts**. We can then use those counts as a new distribution to compute how often we would have seen the features activated. This part is the E step of the EM algorithm. In the end, we normalize our fractional counts to transform them back into probability distributions. These should explain the data a bit better, that is, when we compute the likelihood that these parameters generated the data ($P(y)$ and $P(X|y)$), it should be higher than when we started.

We can repeat the E and M steps indefinitely. Each time, we will get a little bit better in terms of data likelihood, but at some point, it will no longer make a difference. To measure that, we can compute the difference between the data likelihood of the previous iteration and the current one. When that difference is smaller than some threshold, we stop. Alternatively, we can run the steps for a fixed number of iterations, stopping when we reach it. In practice, people typically combine both methods: they set a maximum number of iterations but also measure the data likelihood.

10 Model Bias

Models are their own source of biased predictions. Concretely, we call the tendency of a model to rely on minor differences between subjects to satisfy the objective function and make reasonable predictions **overamplification**. Unchecked, the model can maximize its objective score by amplifying the difference when predicting new data, creating a larger imbalance than in the original data. Essentially, the model might give the correct answers but for the wrong reasons. Yatskar et al. (2016) have shown that in an image-captioning data set, 58 percent of the captions for pictures of a person in a kitchen mentioned women. However, as Zhao et al. (2017) showed, a standard statistical model trained on this slightly biased data ended up predicting the gender of a person in a kitchen picture to be a woman in 63 percent of the cases, a small but noticeable difference, which could be corrected by sampling.

The cost of these false positives seems low. A user might be puzzled or amused when seeing a mislabeled image or receiving an email addressing them with the wrong gender. However, relying on models that produce false positives may lead to **bias confirmation** and **overgeneralization**. Some of these false positives might amuse us, but would we accept them if the system predicted sexual orientation and religious views rather than age and gender? For any text prediction task, this is just a matter of changing the target variable and finding some data.

Another problem of overamplification is the proliferation of stereotypes. Rudinger et al. (2018) found that coreference resolution systems (which link a pronoun to the noun it refers to) were biased by gender. In the sentence, "The surgeon could not operate on her patient: it was her son," the model does not link "surgeon" and "her." The cause of this inability is presumably biased training data, but the effect feeds into gender stereotypes. Similarly, Kiritchenko and Mohammad (2018) showed that sentiment analysis models changed their scores for the same sentences when the researchers replaced a single word, for example, replacing a female with a male pronoun or replacing a typically "white" name with a typically "Black" name. Both "She/He made me feel afraid" and "I made Heather/Latisha feel angry" result in higher scores for the second case.

10.1 Countermeasures

To address the overgeneralization of models, we can ask ourselves, "Would a false answer be worse than no answer?" Instead of taking a *tertium non datur* approach to classification, where a model has to (and will) produce *some* answer, we can use dummy variables that say "unknown." We can also use measures such as error weighting, which incur a higher penalty if the model makes mistakes on the smaller class. Alternatively, we can use confidence thresholds below which we do not assign a label.

Recently, Li et al. (2018) have shown that **adversarial learning** (a specialized architecture in neural networks) can reduce the effect of predictive biases. It even helps improve the performance of the models!

11 Feature Selection

We have our data; we have decided on a classifier; and we have made sure it does not overfit. However, we are not sure these choices have maximized performance. Can we do more to improve it?

If we are using a BOW representation and a linear model, we can fit a classifier (with regularization) and then inspect the magnitude of the coefficients. This **feature selection** can assist us in improving performance by choosing a smaller, more informative set of features. Naturally, if we use feature selection to improve performance, we have to do it on the training data. We cannot peek at the development or the test data!

Analyzing features can also give us an exploratory overview of the correlation between our features and the target class. This correlation can help us discover new facts about the data. For example, correlation can reveal which words best describe each political candidate in a primary

(see `www.washingtonpost.com/news/monkey-cage/wp/2016/02/24/`
`these-6-charts-show-how-much-sexism-hillary-clinton-faces-`
`on-twitter`).

11.1 Dimensionality Reduction

Dimensionality reduction is useful in the context of visualization, and methods like multidimensional scaling, singular value decomposition (SVD), or
nonnegative matrix factorization are often used to plot high-dimensional data
by reducing it to two or three dimensions. However, we can also use dimensionality reduction to improve our performance.

Rather than fitting our model on a large number of features, we can use
dimensionality reduction techniques. Doing so allows us to find a smaller number of dimensions that still capture the variation in the data but provide fewer
chances to overfit by exploiting spurious patterns. This lower-dimensional
representation could, for example, be the U matrix from SVD (see Hovy, 2020).

If we use a lower-dimensional version of a BOW matrix, the individual
dimensions will no longer mean anything – that is, in this version of our matrix,
the columns will no longer be counts or TFIDF values. We will not be able to
map them back to the terms we used as features.

11.2 Chi-Squared

χ^2 (or chi-squared) is a test that measures the correlation between a positive
feature and the categorical outcome variable.

In `sklearn`, we can use the `feature_selection` package to implement the
selection process with χ^2 by sorting the features according to their correlation,
keeping only the top k.

```
1  from sklearn.feature_selection import SelectKBest
2  from sklearn.feature_selection import chi2
3
4  selector = SelectKBest(chi2, k=1500).fit(X, y)
5  X_sel = selector.transform(X)
6  print(X_sel.shape)
```

Code 19 Selecting the top 1,500 features according to their χ^2 value

11.3 Randomized Regression

Logistic regression is a generalized linear model in which the log odds of
the response probability is a linear function of the independent variables. The
coefficients of these variables are estimated via maximum likelihood and are

subsequently interpreted. If we use the model on word-count data and a target category, we can analyze the importance of individual terms by inspecting the magnitude of their coefficients.

However, this approach presupposes that we have already selected the independent variables. In the case of text, the vocabulary size, and therefore the number of independent variables, can be massive. Yet the individual occurrences of terms are sparse (some words occur only once even in large corpora). It is often impossible to know a priori which variables to select.

Luckily, there are several ways to select a subset of informative variables, though each comes with its own limitations: We can remove variables with nonsignificant co-occurrence statistics; however, this requires a large data set and does not guarantee the best model. We can fit all possible models on the entire data and pick the one with the best fit, using some measure of fitness; however, the large number of possible models makes this approach prohibitively extensive computationally, and it is not robust to overfitting. We can fit a model on the entire data set and use an L1 penalty term as an additional constraint that causes uninformative variables to receive 0 weight during fitting; however, this method is highly reliant on extensive data and sufficient observations. Using all of these methods together can help compensate for their individual limitations. For example, to address the last concern, we can randomize the previous method: collect repeated random subsets of the data, fit an L1-penalized (lasso) model to each, and aggregate the coefficient vectors. We can then select variables that frequently receive a high coefficient. When the target variable is binary, this process is randomized logistic regression (or stability selection, see Meinshausen & Bühlmann [2010])

Intuitively, we select variables by simulating a range of different conditions and picking the ones that are informative independent of the condition. In practice, we fit 200–1,000 independent logistic regression models on the data, each on a random subset sampled with replacement. For each model, we use a different weight for the L1 regularization parameter, controlling how aggressively coefficients are driven to 0. Variables that have a score of at least 0.3 (i.e., they received a positive coefficient weight in over 30 percent of the models) can be considered informative. A free online implementation of randomized logistic regression for text, using simple Excel sheets as input, is available at `https://wordify.unibocconi.it`

```
1 from sklearn.linear_model import LogisticRegression
2 import numpy as np
3
```

```
4  def positive_indicatorsRLR(X, y, target, vectorizer,
      selection_threshold=0.3, num_iters=100):
5      n_instances, n_feats = X.shape
6
7      pos_scores = [] # all coefficient > 0
8      neg_scores = [] # all coefficient < 0
9      # choices for lambda weight
10     penalities = [10,5,2,1,0.5,0.1,0.05,0.01,0.005,0.001,0.0001,
          0.00001]
11
12     # select repeated subsamples
13     for iteration in range(num_iters):
14         # initialize a model with randomly-weighted L1 penalty
15         clf = LogisticRegression(penalty='l1', C=penalities[np.
          random.randint(len(penalities))])
16
17         # choose a random subset of indices of the data with
          replacement
18         selection = np.random.choice(n_instances, size=int(
          n_instances * 0.75))
19         try:
20             clf.fit(X[selection], y[selection])
21         except ValueError:
22             continue
23
24         # record which coefficients got a positive or negative score
25         pos_scores.append(clf.coef_ > 0)
26         neg_scores.append(clf.coef_ < 0)
27
28     # normalize the counts
29     pos_scores = (np.array(pos_scores).sum(axis=0)/num_iters).
          reshape(-1)
30     neg_scores = (np.array(neg_scores).sum(axis=0)/num_iters).
          reshape(-1)
31
32     # find the features corresponding to the non-zero
          coefficients
33     features = vectorizer.get_feature_names()
34     pos_positions = [i for i, v in enumerate(pos_scores >=
          selection_threshold) if v]
35     neg_positions = [i for i, v in enumerate(neg_scores >=
          selection_threshold) if v]
36
37     pos = [(features[i], pos_scores[i]) for i in pos_positions]
38     neg = [(features[i], neg_scores[i]) for i in neg_positions]
39
40     posdf = pd.DataFrame(pos, columns='term score'.split()).
          sort_values('score', ascending=False)
41     negdf = pd.DataFrame(neg, columns='term score'.split()).
          sort_values('score', ascending=False)
42
43     return posdf, negdf
```

Code 20 Randomized regression for variable selection

12 Structured Prediction

Imagine you are looking at a collection of legal proceedings. You know that they each follow a certain structure: a *preamble*, followed by an *opening*, followed by a case *description*, which can itself contain various subparts, before concluding with a *decision* and its *justification*. The length of each of these parts is variable, and not all of them need to be there. However, their order is more or less fixed, so once you have found the end of one part, you know the next has to start. You would like to isolate the description and justification. How can you do that?

Alternatively, you might have a hierarchical label scheme for documents. Are they offensive or not? If yes, are they intentionally so? Which group are they targeting? If they are non-offensive, do they contain in-group language? This classification scheme can be expressed via a flow diagram or a tree. Some of these labels (intent, group targeted, and in-group language) only apply if others do, so some of the content and decisions are shared. But not all documents will have all labels.[8] Does it make sense to train a series of classifiers and connect them with `if` clauses?

In all of the previous sections, we have looked at documents as individual elements. A document was either a word on its own or a sentence as the sum of its words. In classification, we try to find the best single label for this input.

However, one of the core properties of language is that it is sequential. We perceive words to follow each other and to each have a position in a sentence. What if we want to find a sequence of labels, one for each word in the sentence? Say we have a sentence like "They can can cans," and we want to find the parts of speech (noun, verb, adjective, etc.) for each word. This task is called **POS tagging** and was one of the early success stories of NLP.

We could just try to generate all possible tag sequences for the sentence (see Figure 9) and use each of those unique sequences as a possible label in a classification task. But there is a problem.

Say each word has on average 1.2 tags, and a sentence has 17 words, like this one. That's 1.2^{17}, or about 22, possible labels. For just one short sentence! Some sentences have 40 or more words, meaning 1,470 or more unique labels. We have to add up all those unique labels. Clearly, we cannot afford to do that, or we would end up with a 10,000-way classification. We will have to do something else.

---

[8] This scheme is a simplified version of the one Sap et al. (2020) implemented, which also included the generation of explanations.

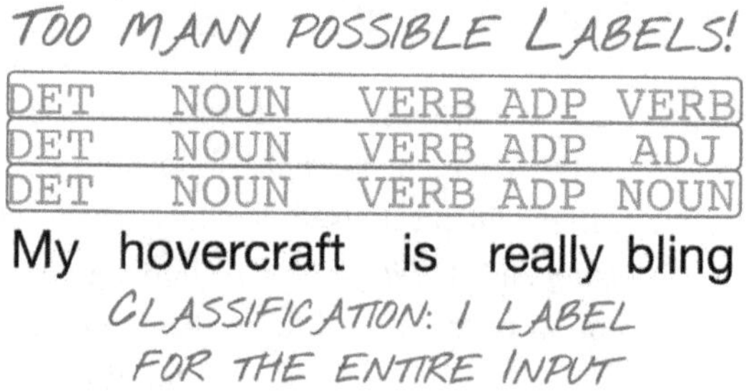

TOO MANY POSSIBLE LABELS!

DET	NOUN	VERB	ADP	VERB
DET	NOUN	VERB	ADP	ADJ
DET	NOUN	VERB	ADP	NOUN

My hovercraft is really bling

CLASSIFICATION: 1 LABEL
FOR THE ENTIRE INPUT

Figure 9 Naive listing of all possible tag sequences

The sequence is also important in grammatical and semantic long-range dependencies. Nouns can occur both before and after verbs. They act either as the subject of a sentence or as its object, that is, either as the thing doing the action (the verb) or as the thing something is done to. For example, the subject-verb agreement (here, *er* and *begegnet*) in this German sentence:

> Wenn er aber auf der Strasse der in Sammt und Seide gehüllten jetzt sehr ungenirt nach der neusten Mode gekleideten Regierungsräthin begegnet.[9]

Such long-range dependencies are also important for relation extraction. Say we wanted to extract the fact founded_by(Amazon, Jeff Bezos) from the sentence, "Jeff Bezos, or what Dr. Evil would look like on steroids, went from book seller to billionaire after he founded Amazon in 1994." The relevant parts are far apart, and we would have to completely ignore the inserted clause. Dependency is also important to determine the **scope** of the negation in "This is *not* in any sense of the word a *funny* movie."

The NLP tools that extract the syntactic structure and the dependencies between words are called **dependency parsers**. While common in many NLP applications, they have yet to become common in the social sciences. Exceptions are studies such as Park et al. (2018), which explicitly took syntactic structure into account to find attitudes toward various human rights; Lucy et al. (2020), in which the authors used dependency parsers to find adjectival phrases that identify marginalized groups; or Atalay et al. (2019), which took the syntactic complexity of sentences into account when predicting the persuasiveness of a marketing communication.

All of these examples are cases for **structured prediction**. In structured prediction, we want to find the best sequence of labels, given a sequence of words.

---

[9] The example is from Mark Twain's essay *The Awful German Language*, and it's slightly old-fashioned but only slightly exaggerated.

The sequential nature of sentences makes words **context-dependent**: They can mean very different things, depending on the context in which they occur. They are **ambiguous**. In the sentence "I will see the show tonight," the word "show" is a noun. However, in the sentence "Let me show you something," the same word is a verb. To decide on the best label for each word, we have to take the context into account.

There are some regularities that help us. Examples of "show" as a noun include sentences like "His show was cancelled" or "We went to see a show together." Other examples of "show" as a verb are "She wanted to show that she could do it" or "They show us a good time."

Even though the words are all different, there are some regularities in the tags of the preceding words. In both cases of "show" as a noun, the preceding word is a determiner. In both cases of the verb "to show," the preceding word is a pronoun (see Hovy, 2020 for details on parts of speech).

To determine the part of speech of a specific word, we need to look at the parts of speech of the preceding words. Of course, their parts of speech, in turn, depend on their preceding words' parts of speech, which depend on *their* preceding words' parts of speech and so on. This is starting to look like infinite recursion.

There are, however, two facts that can help us break the recursion cycle. The first has to do with unambiguous words. Many words have only one possible tag. Not only does that make prediction extremely trivial, it also helps us find regularities in tag sequences. The second is that there is a natural end to the infinite recursion: if we go back far enough, we reach the first word of a sentence. And the tag history of all first words is the same: we can imagine that the sentence beginning has its own unambiguous special tag, say *START*.

These two facts together give us a good starting point to tackle the structured prediction problem. Guess the tag for the first word, given that the previous tag was START, and then proceed in the same manner for each word (see Figure 10).

12.1 The Structured Perceptron

The algorithm that implements this intuition is the **structured perceptron** (Collins, 2002). The central prediction problem it solves can be expressed mathematically as

$$T|W = \arg\max_{Y \in \mathcal{Y}} \sum_{d=1}^{D} \theta_d \cdot \Phi_d(W, Y)$$

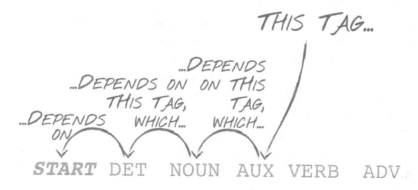

SOME WORDS ARE UNAMBIGUOUS (= ONLY ONE
POSSIBLE TAG)
THE START OF A SENTENCE IS UNAMBIGUOUS

Figure 10 Imagining a START tag for the sentence beginning helps

In other words, we are given a sequence of words, W (a vector of N words, $w_1, w_2, \ldots, w_N$). If we are searching the best tag sequence T (which is a vector of tags $t_1, t_2, \ldots, t_N$), we return the best label sequence Y (out of all possible label sequences $\mathcal{Y}$). To get Y, we compute the sum of all features, Φ, multiplied with their respective weight, θ.

Each of those features is the result of a function that examines W and the predicted tags Y.

$$\Phi_d(W, Y) = \sum_{i=1}^{N} \phi_d(w_i, t_{i-2}, t_{i-1}, W, i)$$

The global features of a sentence, Φ, are simply the sum of all the local features, ϕ_i, derived from the words $w_1, w_2, \ldots, w_N$. Each local feature is derived from the word w_i, the two previous (true or predicted) tags t_{i-2}, t_{i-1}, and the sentence as a whole (W), plus an indicator of the position, i.

To set the weights, we update each θ_d after each sentence, moving the weight closer to the features derived from the true label sequence and further away from the predicted ones:

$$\theta_d = \theta_d + \Phi_d(W, T) - \Phi_d(W, Y)$$

If the features on the predicted tags are the same as the features of the true tags, we don't need to update.

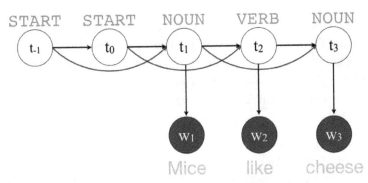

Figure 11 A second-order hidden Markov model

While the math can look intimidating, the algorithm itself is relatively simple. In pseudocode, it only takes a few lines:

```
1  for each iteration:
2      for words, true_tags in examples:
3          features = get_features(words, true_tags)
4          prediction = predict(features)
5          if prediction != true_tags:
6              for feature in features:
7                  weights[feature][true_tags] += 1
8                  weights[feature][prediction] -= 1
```

Code 21 Pseudocode for the structured perceptron

The Structure: Hidden Markov Models

The assumed structure underlying the algorithm is a second-order **hidden Markov model** (HMM). HMMs are used in a variety of applications, but they follow a very simple idea. What we can see (the words) was generated by something we cannot see (the tag sequence), one step at a time, that is, someone first created a sequence of tags and then turned each of them into a word. This is our **generative story**. It sounds a bit strange (this is not how we usually form sentences), but it captures the notion that many sentences have the same syntactic structure.

Assuming an HMM structure helps us model the effect of previous tags. Each tag is influenced by the ones that came before it – one of the so-called **Markov properties**. To make things easier, we assume that each state depends only on *some* of the previous ones, not *all* of them. In a second-order HMM, each tag depends on the two previous states (see Figure 11). This history dependence is the **Markov chain** part of HMMs. What makes it a HMM is the assumption that these tags are unobservable.

You might wonder why we need to make all of these assumptions. Why don't we just take the best tag for each word and be done? Remember that words are ambiguous: The most likely tag for "can" is one of NOUN, VERB, or AUX. But what is the most likely tag for "the can"? Probably no longer VERB or AUX. The context disambiguates it. That's why we want the Markov chain of hidden tags.

The tags are hidden, but they are connected to something we can observe, namely, the words. And that connection follows certain regularities we can capture with features: words ending in "–ing" are more likely to be nouns or verbs; words starting with an uppercase letter are probably proper names and so on. (Note that we also assume that previous words do not influence the current word. This is another Markov property, the independence of the observations from one another.)

Assuming an underlying structure like an HMM, lets us reverse-engineer our generative story, which in turn gives us the most likely sequence of tags. That is what the inference in the structured perceptron uncovers. We reward good features that result in the right tags by increasing their weight, and we decrease the weight of bad features.

12.1.1 Inference

We can choose between two inference algorithms to get the prediction we need to update our weights. The first algorithm is **greedy inference**. It is fast but gives only approximate solutions. Still, in practice, those solutions are pretty good. Greedy inference chooses the highest-scoring tag as a prediction at each step, then moves on. It can therefore be tripped up in longer dependencies.

The second inference algorithm, **Viterbi decoding**, does take context explicitly into account. It chooses each tag based on its score and the score of its best predecessor (which in turn is computed by the same approach). Viterbi decoding is exact and can work better than greedy inference if we have little data. However, it is more involved and therefore slower.

For either inference, we make use of unambiguous words to speed up the process and to avoid errors that could affect accuracy further on.

Greedy Inference

In greedy inference, we look at each word in turn. We derive its features from the tag history, context, and word itself and use them to compute the scores for each possible tag. We pick the highest-scoring tag for this word as output, and then we move on. The tag we just predicted now becomes part of the tag history for the next word. Because it is a series of simple decisions, we can move quickly through a text using greedy inference. All we have to do is iterate over the words. The pseudocode is short and simple:

```
1 for each words, tags:
2     predictions = []
3     for each word in words:
4         scores = get_features(word, tags[-2], tags[-1], words) *
          weights
5         tag = argmax(scores)
6         predictions.append(tag)
```

Code 22 Pseudocode for greedy inference decoding

Despite its efficiency, the greedy inference is not infallible. If we make a wrong decision early in the sentence, it sticks with us. In fact, it becomes the basis of future predictions, which could be affected by this decision. For example, in the sentence, "Attack was their only option," the word "attack" could be labeled as VERB, which would change the scores for subsequent predictions. In practice, though, the greedy inference is fairly robust. It was used in the early taggers of spacy, which was famous for its speed and accuracy.

Viterbi Decoding

The Viterbi inference is slightly more involved than the greedy inference. For each word, we compute a joint score that consists of the regular feature score and the score we computed for the best previous tag. We always carry this history around, and only if we find the best score for the current word do we decide on the best tag for the previous word. That lag allows us to fix mistakes. It does, however, require some overhead in bookkeeping – and a few extra loops.

Since we essentially compute a path through the sentence, going from tag to tag, we use a structure called a lattice or trellis: an interwoven band of paths through the sentence. To keep track of the score and the best predecessor tag, we use two matrices with the same dimensions. Both have one row for each tag in our tag set and one column for each token in our sentence.

The scoring matrix is often called Q. $Q[i,j]$ denotes the score of the best paths leading us up to node word j with tag i. Since we do not need to find the best predecessor for the first word (it's START), the first column of Q is always just the scores of the different tags given the START history. In each subsequent column, each cell is the sum of all best paths arriving there, that is, each tag score multiplied by the Q of the best predecessor (see Figure 12).

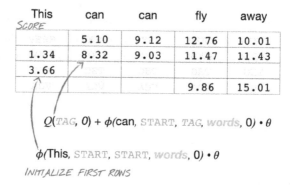

Figure 12 Initialization of Q matrix in Viterbi decoding

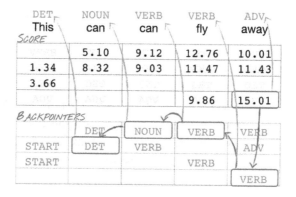

Figure 13 Decoding via backpointers in Viterbi inference

The backpointer matrix (or lattice) has the same shape, but it is a lookup table. The value k in the cell at position i and j tells us that if we tag word j with tag i, the best predecessor tag is k (for word $j - 1$).

We first walk through the sentence, filling the Q and backpointer matrices. For each position, we need to iterate over all possible tags of the previous two positions and to compute the combined score of the current tag and the best predecessor. This is where the tag dictionary for words comes in handy. We only have to iterate over all tags when we get an unknown word.

Once we have reached the end of the sentence, we find the highest-scoring tag for the last token and add it to the output. We then look up the corresponding best predecessor to that tag and, from there, simply follow the backpointers, adding each to the output (see Figure 13). Since we walk through the sentence backward, we need to reverse the result before returning it.

```
1 # initialize scores
2 features = get_features(words[0], START, START, context, 1)
```

```
3  scores = get_scores(features)
4
5  for each allowed tag on word 1:
6      Q[tag, word] = scores[tag]
7
8  # fill lattice for every position and tag with Viterbi score Q
9  for each word i:
10     for each allowed prev_tag on prev_word:
11         best_score = float('-Inf')
12         # score of previous tag on previous word
13         prev_score = Q[prev_tag, prev_word]
14
15         for each allowed prev2_tag:
16             if i == 1:
17                 prev2_tag = START
18
19             # get features of word i with the two previous tags
20             features = get_features(word, prev2_tag, prev_tag,
       context, i)
21             scores = get_scores(features)
22
23             # update best score
24             for each allowed tag on current word:
25                 tag_score = prev_score + scores[tag]
26
27                 if tag_score > best_score:
28                     Q[tag, word] = tag_score
29                     best_score = tag_score
30                     backpointers[tag, word] = prev_tag
31
32 # find best tag for last word
33 best_tag = argmax(Q[:, -1])
34 prediction = [best_tag]
35
36 for i in range(N-1,0,-1):
37     next = backpointers[best_tag, i]
38     prediction.append(next)
39     best_tag = next
40
41 return reversed(prediction)
```

Code 23 Pseudocode for Viterbi decoding

As you can see, the pseudocode is more involved and has more levels of loops. However, the last line in the main loop, where we set the backpointers, is what makes this inference powerful: we decide on the best tag for a word only after we have seen the next one.

The entire code for the structured perceptron adds a few convenience functions for saving and loading trained models, some bookkeeping structures, and output.

The full code is available on the Github page `https://github.com/dirkhovy/text_analysis_for_social_science`. It follows the paper by Collins (2002), with some updates for greedy inference from the Explosion blog post by Matthew Honnibal (`https://explosion.ai/blog/part-of-speech-pos-tagger-in-python`).

Two functions to point out are `get_features()` and `get_scores()`. The first derives all features from a word, its tag history, and the general context. This includes all possible combinations and analyses and can be extended. Nothing in the code is specific to POS tagging, though it might be necessary to add other features for other tasks. To allow both greedy and Viterbi inference, we use a helper function that sums up all word features to a global feature vector for the sentence.

The scoring function takes the features as input. For each feature, it iterates over all tags and looks up the weights associated with this feature for the current tag. Summing up the scores for all features for each tag gives us the tag ranking.

The feature weights are averaged, that is, weighted by their respective frequency. This requires some additional bookkeeping but substantially improves performance.

Note that the weights are updated after each sentence, weighted by the learning rate. Because we update so frequently, the weights can be pushed in a certain direction if we see the same features several times in a row. To break this symmetry, we shuffle the order of instances after each iteration.

You might wonder why you should bother with this model, given that there are very powerful neural networks for sequence (which we will cover in the subsequent sections). The structured perceptron might not be as powerful as, say an LSTM, but it has two things going for it. It needs much less data to achieve decent performance, and it is interpretable. We can look at the feature weights and find exactly what features influence the decision.

NEURAL NETWORKS

13 Background of Neural Networks

Imagine you are trying to predict a complex phenomenon, like human behavior. Simple, linear models can help explain what is happening by creating a simpler version of the problem. However, they will not be able to do justice to the complex relationship between inputs and outputs. To better approximate the complexity of the problem, we need a more complex model. Nonlinear models can match the complexity of problems like human behavior – and language

– and are thus much more adept at analyzing them. However, we buy this complexity with a decrease in explainability.

So far, we have relied on simple, linear, feature-based models for prediction. These models perform reasonably well, and they have the added benefit that they can be interpreted. However, linear models can fail if the underlying distribution is inherently nonlinear – and in many language-related studies, this is precisely the case. It is therefore not too surprising that neural models have recently revolutionized language-related tasks, moving from academic designs to production-strength systems. It started with speech processing, which reached almost human voice recognition and speech-to-text capabilities, and continued with a quantum leap in the quality of machine translations. The effect of networks on NLP has variously been compared to a car on a "rabbit in the headlights,"[10] or to a "tsunami" (Manning, 2015). Despite this violent imagery, the net effect on the field has been positive, as it has provided new avenues in prediction and generation (e.g., in chatbots, for picture descriptions, etc.).

In this section, we will look at the currently dominant class of nonlinear models, **neural networks**, which have opened up new ways to do research. They have excellent predictive performance, and they can learn representations, which has freed us from cumbersome **feature engineering**. Instead, they use word embeddings, which has allowed us to spend more time experimenting with model architectures to find those that best capture the underlying problem.

Neural networks are a very active, fast-developing research area. There are new, fundamental developments almost monthly. In 2018, a debate about whether one model type or another was better for text classification took place via conference papers over several months. Recommendations and best practices changed at the same speed. There are plenty more open issues out there, and they grow even more numerous by the day. In order to delve deeply into the nuances of neural networks, we would need much more space than we have here, as the mathematical underpinnings alone require a substantial treatment of various linear algebra concepts. And even then, any explanation we might provide would be largely outdated by the time this appeared. Instead, we will focus on the *intuition* behind neural networks and look at a few select model architectures to give you an idea of the range.

For a more in-depth, excellent introduction to the use of neural networks in NLP, see Goldberg (2017) or the shorter primer on which it is based (Goldberg, 2016). For an intuitive explanation and great visualization,

---

[10] https://inverseprobability.com/2016/05/15/nlp-is-a-rabbit-in-the-headlights

see the excellent videos by 3Blue1Brown at `www.youtube.com/watch?v=aircAruvnKk&list=PLZHQObOWTQDNU6R1_67000Dx_ZCJB-3pi`. For more implementation details in `keras`, see Chollet (2017).

13.1 Neural History

While neural networks have dominated ML news over the last few years, in reality, they are old technology. The first version, the **perceptron**, was inspired by actual neurons and was introduced in the 1950s by Rosenblatt (1958). For an overview of applications in political science, see Chatsiou and Mikhaylov (2020).

While perceptrons were initially greeted with great excitement, there were some early setbacks. It became apparent that the perceptron itself was limited (Minsky & Papert, 1969, proved that perceptrons could not learn the exclusive OR logic function, see later). However, it eventually became clear that this model was a great building block for more complex systems. We can build **layers** by running several simple perceptrons over the same input and using their outputs as input for another perceptron. The resulting model is a **multilayer perceptron** or **feed-forward neural network** (these terms mean the same thing and are used interchangeably). The more layers (i.e., the deeper the stack of layers, hence deep learning), the more expressive the model becomes, the more complex phenomena it can tackle.

Many fields have now seen revolutionary breakthroughs using these neural networks. In NLP, word embeddings have been at the forefront of this progress, which has expanded to include very flexible model architectures. We have seen a lot of innovation, and many tasks have significantly improved. The most publicly visible example of this shift is probably the translation quality of services like Google Translate (Wu et al., 2016).

The one drawback neural networks have for social scientists is their lack of interpretability. As great as they are at correctly predicting an outcome, it is tough to explain why they do so. This problem has the same origin as the networks' strength: their distributed nature. Each level in the architecture specializes during training, and by taking different paths from input to output, we can theoretically model any relationship between them. Computer vision research (an early adopter of neural networks) has shown that different layers in the network correspond to different visual correlates. For example, the first layers recognize lines, then simple shapes, then parts of faces, and ultimately things like generic faces for facial recognition. Unfortunately, for language, matters are less straightforward. The initial hope with networks was that they would mirror the brain and that their layers would correspond to different levels of linguistic analysis, that is, phonology, morphology, syntax, and semantics (Dell, 1986). So far, this has not panned out. Using an architectural feature called **attention** (Bahdanau et al., 2014), we can now at least show the influence of individual words or passages. (It also turns out to be very useful for performance.) However, the use of neural networks for explanation remains minimal. Still, neural networks are a rapidly developing research area, and new algorithms come out constantly.

To better understand the power and potential of networks, we will first review the basics, then introduce elements of networks that have proven useful.

13.2 Network Basics

Generally, neural networks for the prediction can be grouped into four classes based on the type of input and output involved in each (see also Figure 14):

(1) Fixed-length input, fixed-length output: for example, classify a word embedding as dialect or standard. This uses a feed-forward neural architecture such as the **perceptron** (see 13.3).

(2) Variable-length input, fixed-length output: for example, classify a text (i.e., a sequence of word embeddings) as positive, negative, or neutral. This is the use case for **convolutional neural network**s (see 14.1).

(3) Variable-length input, variable-length output: for example, labeling each word with its part of speech, or translating a German text into a French text. This uses **recurrent neural network**s (see 14.2).

(4) Fixed-length input, variable-length output: for example, text generation based on a prompt (this uses a decoder architecture), or the classification of multiple properties of a document embedding (this uses a **multitask learning** architecture).

13.2.1 Training

The basic idea behind training a network is that of show-and-tell. The network is initialized randomly and then presented with input-output pairs. We take the input, run it through the network, and see whether it produces the desired output. The most useful explanation of this process comes from a *New York Times* article on AI (Lewis-Kraus, 2016):

> Imagine that you're playing with a child. You tell the child, "Pick up the green ball and put it into Box A." The child picks up a green ball and puts it into Box B. You say, "Try again to put the green ball in Box A." The child tries Box A. Bravo.

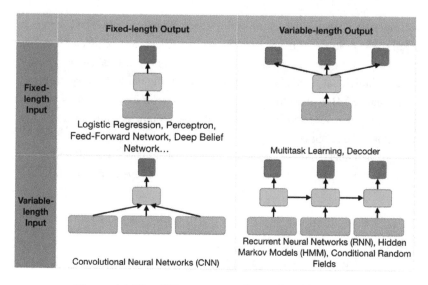

Figure 14 The different types of neural architectures

This example describes a model that only has an input and an output layer. However, as we add more layers to get more power, things get a lot more complicated, especially when the prediction does not match the output. From the same article (emphasis my own):

> Now imagine you tell the child, "Pick up a *green* ball, go through the *door marked 3* and put the green ball into *Box A*." The child takes a **red** ball, goes through the **door marked 2** and puts the red ball into **Box B**. How do you begin to correct the child? You cannot just repeat your initial instructions, because the child does not know at which point he went wrong.

If the prediction does not match the output, we use an **error function** to compute how *different* the prediction was from the intended output. We then walk back from the output through each layer of the network, adjusting the parameters at each step in such a way that they produce the correct output the next time around. This step is called **backpropagation**, and it is what sets the parameters of the model. Obviously, the updates we need to make at each layer depend on the updates we needed to make at each previous layer.

Normally, we stop the backpropagation at the last layer before we reach the input. If instead, we include the input in the updating process, we are essentially also learning the best way to represent the problem for the task, that is, through embeddings. This part is therefore called **representation learning** (if we started with random embeddings) or **fine-tuning** (if we use existing embeddings).

$$f(X) = a(w_1 x_1 + w_2 x_2 + b) \qquad \hat{y} = \begin{cases} +1 & \text{if } f(X) \geq 0 \\ -1 & \text{otherwise} \end{cases}$$

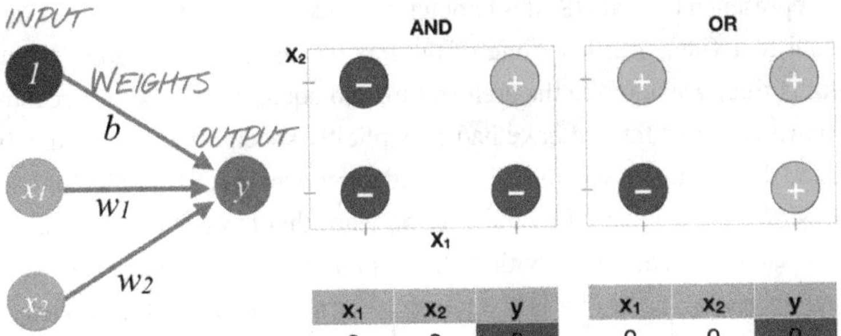

X_1	X_2	y
0	0	0
1	0	0
0	1	0
1	1	1

X_1	X_2	y
0	0	0
1	0	1
0	1	1
1	1	1

Figure 15 Visualizations, logical tables, architecture, and equations for AND and OR perceptrons

During backpropagation, we have to compute what went wrong at each layer (e.g., ball color, door, box). Then we can tell the previous layer what parameters it has to correct in order to give the current layer the right input. What model parameters do we optimize in backpropagation? As we will see, they are simply vectors and matrices of weights.

13.3 The Perceptron

The grandfather and basic building block of any neural network is the perceptron (Rosenblatt, 1958). The perceptron was inspired by the observation that actual neurons fire when they receive a signal that exceeds a certain threshold. We can also imagine this (maybe less grandiosely, but more aptly) like a smoke detector. It has an array of sensors (say, one on each side, or maybe at different heights), and it sums up the readings from all of them. If the total amount of smoke measured exceeds a certain limit, it rings the alarm. The perceptron works similarly: it weighs the information from the different inputs, and if their total information crosses a threshold, it produces an output.

Rosenblatt (1958) showed that a perceptron with two binary inputs and one binary output could learn to solve simple logic functions like AND and OR (see Figure 15 for visualization and the logical tables of both) with the same basic architecture. The input value for each node is simply 0 or 1, and the output of the perceptron is +1 or −1.

To represent a logical AND, the perceptron checks whether the sum of the weighted inputs equals 2. If it does, that means both input nodes were on (or true); therefore, the output is true, and the perceptron outputs $+1$.

To represent a logical OR, it is enough to check whether the sum of the inputs is equal to 1 (i.e., if at least one of the inputs was true). If it does, then the output is true. You can see the architecture and equations for both perceptrons in Figure 15. Thus far, we have had to explicitly specify the threshold, which changed depending on whether we wanted to recognize AND or OR functions. It turns out that we can let the perceptron learn that threshold, allowing us to use the same perceptron for both AND and OR functions. To do that, we first add another input node that is always on (which is called the **bias term**). The bias node has its own bias weight, which corresponds to the threshold needed for the respective functions.

The summed value from all the inputs is now a linear combination of the two input values, each multiplied with their respective weight, plus the bias term (which is the input value 1 multiplied by its bias weight). We can write this value as a function over the inputs X, which is a vector with the input values x_1 and x_2:

$$f(X) = w_1 x_1 + w_2 x_2 + b$$

However, we still need to test whether $f(X)$ exceeds a certain threshold. Since we could have weights of any size, $f(X)$ could have almost any value. To get it back into a defined range, we use a special function that limits the possible range to a minimum and maximum. No matter how large or small $f(X)$ is, it can never exceed that range. That is, we squeeze the result of $f(X)$ to be within the desired range. This squeezing results in an S-like curve if we plot all values of $f(X)$ and their squeezed value. There are different functions available that achieve this S shape, and they are jointly referred to as **sigmoid functions**. Some of them are shown in Figure 16.

Depending on which sigmoid function we choose, the range can be from -1 to 1, or from 0 to 1. Once we have such a defined range, our threshold simply becomes the midpoint between the minimum and maximum value. For example, if we use the hyperbolic tangent (*tanh*) function, which squeezes everything into a range from -1 to 1, our threshold becomes 0. The original perceptron used a logistic function as sigmoid, which ranges from 0 to 1.

Once we have that threshold value, anything above it is the positive output class, everything below, the negative output class. Our prediction $\hat{y}$ is $+1$ if we are above the threshold, and -1 if we are below it. Applying the sigmoid transformation of $f(x)$ and testing whether it exceeds the threshold for the perceptron to fire is called an **activation function**.

$$f(X) = a(w_1 x_1 + w_2 x_2 + b)$$

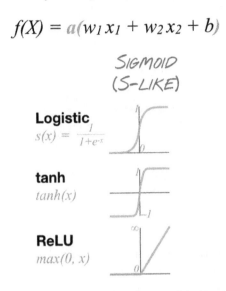

Figure 16 Activation functions and their output

Rosenblatt's discovery of an architecture able to learn *both* logical AND and OR functions, simply by learning the appropriate threshold for each from the data, got people very excited about the possibilities of perceptrons.

It got even more exciting when it turned out that the perceptron could do more than just learn AND and OR functions. Its weights essentially define a decision boundary between positive and negative examples. People began to realize that they could use the perceptron to predict the labels of new data!

The problem was that this simple architecture broke down when faced with the *exclusive or* (XOR) problem: a case in which the output is only true if one input is true and the other one false. If both are true or both are false, then the output is false. No matter how you choose the threshold, you can never produce the right output for all inputs. This is an example of a **linearly non-separable** problem. We cannot draw a decision boundary between the examples of different classes. This result from Minsky & Papert (1969) dealt the perceptron and the development of AI a major blow. Excitement abated, and the development of AI stalled for a while.

Marsland (2011) has a friendly introduction to the perceptron and neural networks in Python.

```
1 import numpy as np
2
3 def sigmoid(x):
```

```
4      '''
5      ranges from  0 to 1
6      '''
7      return 1 / (1 + np.exp(-x))
8
9  class Perceptron:
10     def __init__(self, num_inputs):
11         # initialize the weights randomly, and set the bias to 1
12         self.w1 = np.random.random(num_inputs)
13         self.b1 = 1
14
15     def predict(self, X):
16         # compute activation for input layer
17         fX = np.dot(X, self.w1) + self.b1
18         # non-linear transform
19         activation = sigmoid(fX)
20         # check threshold: for sigmoid, use 0.5, for tanh, use 0
21         y = np.where(fX >= 0.5, 1, -1)
22         return y
23
24     def fit(self, train_data, train_labels, num_epochs=20):
25         models = []
26         print(num_epochs)
27         for epoch in range(1, num_epochs+1):
28             print(epoch)
29             for (X, y) in zip(train_data, train_labels):
30                 pred_label = self.predict(X)
31
32                 if pred_label != y:
33                     print('update')
34                     self.w1 = self.w1 + (X * y)
35                     self.b1 = self.b1 + y
36
37             models.append((self.w1, self.b1))
38
39         return models
```

Code 24 A simple perceptron implementation

We can use this perceptron to fit the basic logic functions it was originally developed to match.

```
1  and_data = np.array([[1, 1], [1, 0], [0, 1], [0, 0]])
2  and_labels = np.array([1, -1, -1, -1])
3
4  or_data = np.array([[1, 1], [1, 0], [0, 1], [0, 0]])
5  or_labels = np.array([1, 1, 1, -1])
6
7  xor_data = np.array([[1, 1], [1, 0], [0, 1], [0, 0]])
8  xor_labels = np.array([-1, 1, 1, -1])
9
10 # initialize perceptron
11 perceptron = Perceptron(2)
```

```
12
13 iters = perceptron.fit(and_data, and_labels, num_epochs=10)
14 and_predictions = perceptron.predict(and_data)
```

Code 25 Fitting a perceptron on simple logic functions

Obviously, this version is somewhat overly simple. To make it more powerful and flexible, we can use the `keras` library in Python.

```
 1 from keras.models import Model
 2 from keras.layers import Input, Dense
 3
 4 # input: a sequence  of 2 integers
 5 main_input = Input(shape=(2,), name='main_input')
 6
 7 # add the output layer
 8 output = Dense(2, activation='hard_sigmoid', name='output',
        kernel_initializer='glorot_uniform')(main_input)
 9
10 # f(X) = sigmoid(X*W + b)
11
12 # the model is specified by connecting input and output
13 perceptron_keras = Model(inputs=[main_input], outputs=[output])
14
15 # compile the model
16 perceptron_keras.compile(loss='binary_crossentropy',
17                 optimizer='sgd',
18                 metrics=['accuracy'])
19
20 # train the model on a validation set and dave the loss and
        accuracy for every epoch
21 history = perceptron_keras.fit(X, y,
22                 epochs=15,
23                 verbose=1,
24                 validation_split=0.2
25         )
```

Code 26 perceptron implementation in the `keras` functional API

13.4 The Multilayer Perceptron

We can graph the two inputs and the resulting output for the AND and OR problems, as in Figure 15. We can see that the two output classes can be separated by drawing a straight line (called the **decision boundary**). However, for the XOR problem, we cannot draw any linear decision boundary that separates the two output classes (see Figure 17). The operative word for the decision boundary in the XOR problem turns out to be *linear*. To overcome the XOR problem, the model needed to use a more flexible decision boundary. We cannot use a

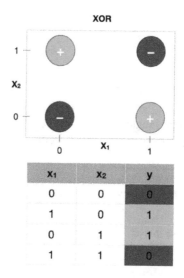

Figure 17 Visualization and logical table for the XOR function

straight line to separate the classes, but we can use a curve. The problem was how to do this programmatically.

A curve, it turns out, is nothing more than a more complex function. So the solution to the XOR problem was simple. We use several perceptrons, all on the same input, and then add another perceptron on top, which uses the outputs of the first set of perceptrons as input. Because this input to the final perceptron is not "visible" (i.e., it is not part of the problem we are given, but generated by us), it is called a **latent layer**.

The resulting architecture is a lot more complex. It needs a lot more weights, including several bias weights (see Figure 18), but it is capable of solving the XOR problem. In fact, we can theoretically approximate *any* underlying distribution, no matter how complicated it is, by using several nonlinear functions in a row. Because of this property, neural networks are **universal function approximators**, and they have done extremely well in cases where the input and output are indeed connected through a complicated function.

This architecture has other advantages: if we want more than two output classes, we can simply add more (binary) output nodes. The predicted output is then a vector of output scores, and the prediction is simply the ID of the node with the highest activation score.

As you can see from the diagram in Figure 18, these models quickly become a confusing mess of nodes, weights, and their indices. To implement and compute all this efficiently, it is easier to use vectors and matrices. Figure 19 shows

$$f(X) = a_2(V\,a_1(WX + B_1) + B_2)$$

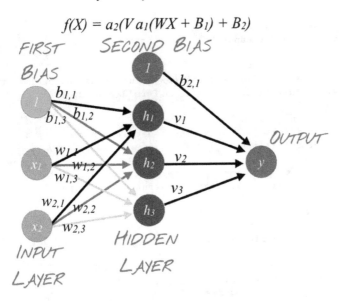

Figure 18 Architecture and equation for the multilayer perceptron

EXPLICIT NOTATION

$$y = a(w_{1,1}x_1 + w_{2,1}x_2 + b_1)$$

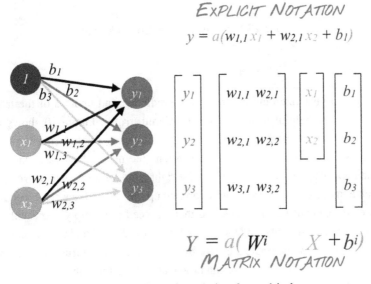

$$Y = a(\ W^i \qquad X + b^i)$$
MATRIX NOTATION

Figure 19 Visualization of matrix notation for multi-class perceptron

what the explicit notation with indices looks like as matrices and in matrix notation. We have already discussed how to represent our input and output as these structures. By representing biases and weights as matrices as well, we can use operations like dot products to quickly calculate the activation, error, or prediction.

```
1  # input: a sequence  of 2 integers
2  mlp_input = Input(shape=(2,), name='main_input')
3
4  # add a hidden layer
5  mlp_hidden = Dense(16, activation='relu', name='hidden',
       kernel_initializer='glorot_uniform')(mlp_input)
6
7  # add the output layer
8  mlp_output = Dense(2, activation='softmax', name='output',
       kernel_initializer='glorot_uniform')(mlp_hidden)
9
10 # the model is specified by connecting input and output
11 mlp = Model(inputs=[mlp_input], outputs=[mlp_output])
12
13 mlp.compile(loss='binary_crossentropy',
14             optimizer='sgd',
15             metrics=['accuracy']
16            )
17
18 mlp_history = mlp.fit(X, y,
19               epochs=50,
20               verbose=1,
21               validation_split=0.2)
```

Code 27 Multilayer perceptron in keras

13.5 Computation

In order to visualize (and compute) the prediction and updates of the train-ing, it can be helpful to use a **computational graph**. Figure 20 shows the steps involved in computing the error for a prediction on the sentence, "You are back." Each circle depicts an operation (the nonmathematical ones are explained). Above each circle and to the right is the resulting vector we oper-ate on at that step. We start out with looking up the embeddings corresponding to the words, concatenate them, and then proceed to multiply them with the respective layer weights, add the biases, and apply a reLU and a softmax func-tion. After that, we compute the error by comparing it to the true answer. Once we have computed the error, we can propagate it back through the graph. Here, we can only provide a general introduction to the mechanics. For a much more detailed explanation, see Goldberg (2017).

13.6 Error Computation

In the perceptron, we updated the weights simply if the prediction did not match the true label. However, that approach works best for binary classification. In modern neural networks, we use more general ways to compute the error.

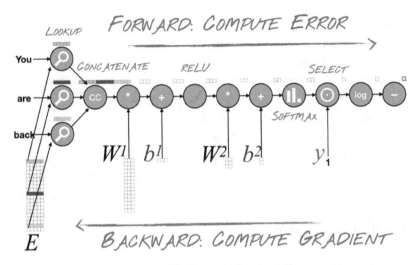

Figure 20 Computational graph

In order to do differential backpropagation, we need to first quantify *how far* we are off in our prediction. One of the most common ways to do so is **cross-entropy**.

We compare the predicted probability distribution over the output labels (from a softmax) with the true answer. The true answer is encoded as a **one-hot** distribution, which is a probability distribution in which all the mass is on one outcome, and all others are set to 0.0.

$$-\sum_{k=1}^{K} \log(\hat{y}_k) * y_k$$

To compute the error, we take each output label k, multiply the logarithm of the predicted likelihood $\hat{y}_k$ by the likelihood of the true answer y_k (i.e., either 0 or 1), sum up all those numbers, and take the negative of the result.

13.7 Dropout

Dropout, simply described, is the concept that if you can learn how to do a task repeatedly whilst drunk, you should be able to do the task even better when sober.

Stephen Merity

We have previously seen how regularization can improve the performance and generalizability of our classifiers. The idea is to make the training more difficult to fit, thereby forcing the model to find a more general explanation. Previously, we have done so by adding an error term that captures the sparsity and norm of the weights. We can still apply this form of regularization in neural networks, but there is another method that has proven effective.

In **dropout** (Hinton et al., 2012), we simply remove a percentage of the nodes at random at each iteration. This forces the model to base its predictions on multiple paths in the network, rather than on one dominant node.

The idea for regularization methods like dropout is motivated by overfitting examples like that of ALVINN (Pomerleau, 1989). ALVINN was a shallow network that was developed to steer an autonomous vehicle. It used input from cameras to learn to predict how the driver should (re)act. After driving the car down a road, the researchers turned it around to drive back – and the car promptly went off the road. It turned out that there was a ditch on one side of the road, which showed up as darker pixels. ALVINN had learned to associate having those darker pixels on one side with keeping direction. But when the car turned around, the ditch was on the other side (Pomerleau, 2012). ALVINN had overfit to the ditch.

Methods like dropout essentially ask networks to do the job even if we take the helpful ditch away. It forces the network to pay attention to other factors (say, the side of the road).

In keras, we can add dropout as activation to any layer, specifying the proportion of nodes to affect.

```
1  dropout = Dropout(0.3, name='dropout')(layer)
```

Code 28 Adding dropout to a layer in keras

We will later see an example of dropout in use (see Code 33).

13.8 Data Preprocessing

In the following section, we will use the keras library to implement networks. keras provides two ways of specifying models: sequentially or functionally. In the sequential API, the sequence in which we specify the layers in the code corresponds to the structure of the network. In the functional API, each layer is a function that operates on the input we give it. The latter is a lot more flexible, as we can add back input from a few layers further down. The examples in this Element will all follow the functional API.

Keras requires some preprocessing of the data to get it into the format the library expects.

```
1  # collect known word tokens and tags
2  wordset, labelset = set(), set()
3
4  # collect all unique labels
```

```
 5 labelset.update(set(train_labels))
 6
 7 # collect all word types in the training data
 8 for words in train_instances:
 9     wordset.update(set(words))
10
11 # map words and tags into integer IDs
12 PAD = '-PAD-'
13 UNK = '-UNK-'
14 word2int = {word: i + 2 for i, word in enumerate(sorted(wordset)
       )}
15 word2int[PAD] = 0  # special token for padding
16 word2int[UNK] = 1  # special token for unknown words
17
18 label2int = {label: i for i, label in enumerate(sorted(labelset)
       )}
19 # structure to translate IDs back to labels
20 int2label = {i:label for label, i in label2int.items()}
21
22 # helper function
23 def convert2ints(instances):
24     result = []
25     for words in instances:
26         # replace words with ID, use 1 for unknown words
27         word_ints = [word2int.get(word, 1) for word in words]
28         result.append(word_ints)
29     return result
30
31 # convert data and labels
32 train_instances_int = convert2ints(train_instances)
33 train_labels_int = [label2int[label] for label in train_labels]
34
35 test_instances_int = convert2ints(test_instances)
36 test_labels_int = [label2int[label] for label in test_labels]
37
38 # convert labels to 1-hot encoding
39 from keras.utils import to_categorical
40 train_labels_1hot = to_categorical(train_labels_int, len(
       label2int))
41 test_labels_1hot = to_categorical(test_labels_int, len(label2int
       ))
```

Code 29 Data preprocessing for use in keras

In theory, we can process inputs of any length with recurrent or convolutional neural networks. In practice, we need to specify the maximum length we expect to see. If we have instances that are longer, they simply get chopped off after that length. Shorter instances will get padded with a special 0 token, which is why we reserve one in preprocessing.

```
1 # compute 95th percentile of training sentence lengths
2 L = sorted(map(len, train_instances))
3 MAX_LENGTH = L[int(len(L) * 0.95)]
```

```
4
5 # apply padding
6 from keras.preprocessing.sequence import pad_sequences
7 train_instances_int = pad_sequences(train_instances_int, padding
      ='post', maxlen=MAX_LENGTH)
8 test_instances_int = pad_sequences(test_instances_int, padding='
      post', maxlen=MAX_LENGTH)
```

Code 30 Computing a maximum length and padding instances up to that amount

14 Neural Architectures and Models

14.1 Convolutional Neural Nets

Multilayer perceptrons or feed-forward neural networks are powerful, but they do have their limitations. The main one is that they can only process inputs of a fixed length: If we set up the architecture to expect an input vector of dimension 300, then we have to stick to this decision. This restriction is unproblematic for classifying words, since we can just use embeddings, but it gets tricky with documents. Of course, we could use document embeddings, but this brings us back to the special properties of language: compositionality and long-range dependencies. In a document embedding or discrete representation, "Not bad, actually quite good" and "Not good, actually quite bad" look very similar. They mean very different things, though! Furthermore, it is impossible to capture long-range dependencies, for example, in relation extraction, in a single vector representation. Instead, we need a way to take an arbitrarily long sequence of word vectors (usually embeddings) and gobble them up to produce a single output.

Not for the first time, the solution to this problem comes from computer vision. To transform an image into a manageable vector, we can move a small window over the image pixel by pixel, from top left to bottom right, and take a snapshot of each position. The result is a smaller set of snapshots. We can then repeat this process until we have the dimensionality we need.

The image is a matrix in which each cell represents a pixel. This matrix is repeated several times to represent the various **channels** (RGB and alpha) that will yield a three-dimensional tensor. In NLP, we only have a matrix: each row is a word embedding (we could have different channels representing different versions of the sentence, for example, translations, but here, we assume a single channel).

Each of the windows, or **regions**, is a word *n*-gram, that is, a smaller matrix. We can have several regions of different sizes (say, bigrams and trigrams) or several copies of the same region size (say, two trigram regions). Each of these smaller matrices is a **filter**. Let's say we have a trigram filter and slide it over the

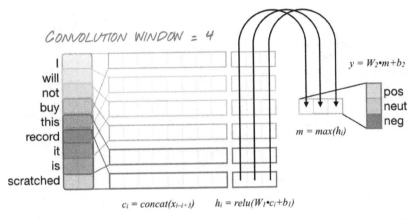

$$c_i = concat(x_{i-i+3}) \qquad h_i = relu(W_1 \cdot c_i + b_1)$$

Figure 21 Text convolution with a filter size of four words and a stride length of one

sentence: Do we go word by word to get overlapping snapshots, or do we move the filter by three words at each step to get adjacent snapshots? This decision is captured in the **stride** length.

Depending on the region size and the stride length, dragging the filter over the sentence produces a number of **feature maps**. For example, in Figure 21, we have one filter with a region size of four and a stride length of one. With nine input words, we get six feature maps. With four input words, we would have only one feature map. If we want, we can run each of these feature maps through an activation function.

We hope that each feature map captures some of the dependencies and compositions in the region, but it still leaves us with a variable output length. To reduce this variable length to a fixed length, we use **pooling**. Simply put, we take the matrix of feature maps and select the maximum value from each of its dimensions. The result is a fixed-length vector: we have essentially squashed the feature map matrix into one row. Note that we could use operations other than the maximum (e.g., the minimum or mean) to pool the outputs. In practice, though, the maximum works best.

In keras, we can implement the various layers in a very straightforward manner:

```
1 from keras.models import Model
2 from keras.layers import Input
3 from keras.layers import Embedding
4 from keras.layers.convolutional import Conv1D
5 from keras.layers import GlobalMaxPooling1D, Dropout
6 from keras.layers.core import Dense, Activation
7 import numpy as np
8 np.random.seed(42)
```

```
 9
10  # set parameters of matrices and convolution
11  embedding_dim = 64
12  nb_filter = 64
13  filter_length = 3
14
15  inputs = Input((MAX_LENGTH, ),
16                  name='word_IDs')
17  embeddings = Embedding(len(word2int),
18                          embedding_dim,
19                          input_length=MAX_LENGTH)(inputs)
20  convolution = Conv1D(filters=nb_filter,  # Number of filters
21                  kernel_size=filter_length, #  stride length
        of each filter
22                  padding='same', #valid: don't go off edge;
        same: use padding before applying filter
23                  activation='relu',
24                  strides=1)(embeddings)
25  pooling = GlobalMaxPooling1D()(convolution)
26  dropout1 = Dropout(0.2)(pooling)
27  dense = Dense(32, activation='relu')(dropout1)
28  dropout2 = Dropout(0.2)(dense)
29  output = Dense(len(label2int), activation='softmax')(dropout2)
30
31  model = Model(inputs=[inputs], outputs=[output])
32  model.compile(optimizer='adam',
33                  loss='binary_crossentropy',
34                  metrics=['accuracy'])
35  model.summary()
```

Code 31 keras implementation of a CNN

We can now compile and run the model on the preprocessed data:

```
 1  # batch size can have a huge effect on performance!
 2  batch_size = 64
 3  epochs = 5
 4
 5  history = model.fit(train_instances_int, train_labels_1hot,
 6                  batch_size=batch_size,
 7                  epochs=epochs,
 8                  verbose=1,
 9                  validation_data=(dev_instances_int,
        dev_labels_1hot)
10                  )
11
12  loss, accuracy = model.evaluate(test_instances_int,
        test_labels_1hot,
13                          batch_size=batch_size,
14                          verbose=False)
15
16  print("\nTesting Accuracy:  {:.4f}".format(accuracy))
```

Code 32 Compiling and fitting a CNN model in keras

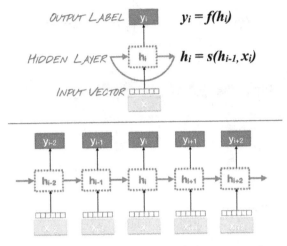

Figure 22 Generic recurrent neural network, in compact form (top) and unrolled (bottom), based on Goldberg (2017)

14.2 Recurrent Neural Nets

Recurrent neural networks are designed to deal with the structured prediction (see above). They assume we have a sequence of inputs, and they produce a sequence of outputs (usually, but not necessarily, the same number as the inputs).

In their most generic form (see Figure 22), they have an input layer, a hidden layer, and an output layer. The hidden layer is a combination of the hidden state of the previous time step and the input at the current time step. The output is simply the result of applying an activation function to the hidden state. Concretely, we could make a linear combination of the input and hidden state, run it through a *tanh* activation function to squash the result into the range between −1 and 1, and output that number. This approach would allow us to make a binary classification at each time step, depending on the previous words. For example, if we wanted to decide at each time step whether a word was English or not English (i.e., code-switching).

One of the most useful applications of RNNs is in language modeling. Instead of predicting some label, we predict at each step which word of the vocabulary should come next (see Figure 23 for an example). This predicted word is then the input to the next time step, and so forth. In essence, an RNN language model feeds itself the next steps. Because we store the information of what has happened before in the hidden state, we can essentially keep an unlimited history around (encoded somehow in the vector representation of the

$$P(w_1, w_2, ..., w_n) \approx \prod_{i=1}^{N} P(w_i|w_1,w_{i-1})$$

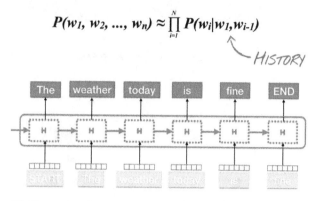

Figure 23 Example of a recurrent neural network language model, with theoretically infinite history

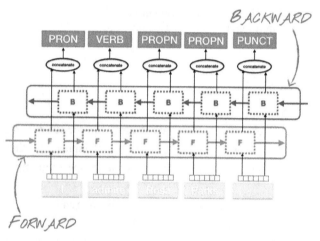

Figure 24 Bidirectional recurrent neural network architecture for POS tagging

hidden state). In contrast, probabilistic language models need to limit themselves to a fixed context (the Markov order of the model). They therefore need to trade off how far back they can look with how many parameters they need. We could have a 15-gram probabilistic language model, but that would require us to keep a huge amount of very sparse *n*-gram probabilities around, which is not very practical.

When we speak, we not only base our next word on what have just said, but also on what we plan to say afterward (Levelt, 1993). It therefore makes sense to model this future dependence in recurrent models. To do that, we run a recurrent neural net on the reversed sentence: we start with the last word and work our way backward. Each hidden state therefore encodes all the words that

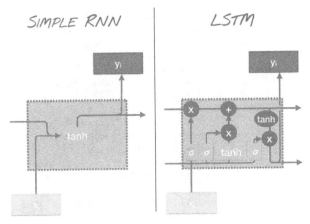

Figure 25 Internal structure of the simple RNN and the LSTM hidden state

come after it. By combining the hidden states of this model with a regular RNN (usually by simply concatenating the two vectors), we get a **bidirectional RNN** (see Figure 24).

Having, in essence, an unlimited memory of the previous words (or the future ones, as we have just seen) is great in theory. In practice, though, it is not always useful. In all the examples of long-range dependencies we have seen so far, there was one word or phrase we needed to remember, but the intervening material was often unrelated and self-contained. So once we have processed an inserted subordinate clause, we need no longer burden our memory with it; all it does is take up space and potentially create confusion. The trick is to know what to keep and what to forget. This was the intuition behind the somewhat oddly named **long short-term memory (LSTM)** (Hochreiter & Schmidhuber, 1997). To achieve this selective memory, the model includes various activation functions and gates (see Figure 25 for a schematic).

In keras, we can implement an LSTM or Bi-LSTM relatively easily.

```
1  from keras.models import Model
2  from keras.layers import Input, Embedding
3  from keras.layers import Bidirectional, LSTM
4  from keras.layers import Dropout, Dense, Activation
5  import numpy as np
6
7  # Set a random seed for reproducibility
8  np.random.seed(42)
9
10 inputs = Input((MAX_LENGTH, ),
11                 name='word_IDs')
12 embeddings = Embedding(input_dim=len(word2int),
13                        output_dim=128,
```

```
14                         mask_zero=True,
15                         name='embeddings')(inputs)
16 lstm = LSTM(units=256,
17                return_sequences=True,
18                name="LSTM")(embeddings)
19 # for a Bi-LSTM, replace the line above with this:
20 # from keras.layers import Bidirectional
21 #bilstm = Bidirectional(LSTM(units=256,
22 #                         return_sequences=True),
23 #                     name="Bi-LSTM")(embeddings)
24 dropout = Dropout(0.3, name='dropout')(lstm)
25 lstm_out = Dense(len(tag2int), name='output')(dropout)
26 output = Activation('softmax', name='softmax')(lstm_out)
27
28 model = Model(inputs=[inputs], outputs=[output])
29 model.summary()
```

Code 33 A (Bi-)LSTM in `keras`

To train the model and log the output, we can use Code 34

```
1 batch_size = 32
2 epochs = 5
3
4 # compile the model we have defined above
5 model.compile(loss='categorical_crossentropy',
6                optimizer='adam',
7                metrics=['accuracy']
8                )
9
10 # run training and capture ouput log
11 history = model.fit(train_sentences, train_tags_1hot,
12                         batch_size=batch_size,
13                         epochs=epochs,
14                         verbose=1,
15                         validation_split=0.2)
```

Code 34 Compiling and training a `keras` model

14.3 Attention

We have repeatedly touched upon the importance of context and the value of selective memory. It turns out that there is a way to combine these two aspects: **attention**. This mechanism was first introduced in machine translation, where it is necessary to align the words in the sentences of the input and output languages. These alignments are not always one-to-one. For example, the English "not" corresponds to a "ne [...] pas" in French. The English dummy "do" (in questions) or the impersonal German "es" (in generic statements) often have no corresponding word in other languages.

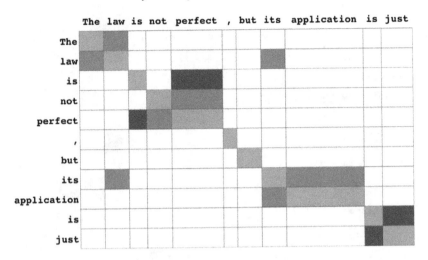

Figure 26 Self-attention in a CNN

To capture these correspondences, Bahdanau et al. (2015) introduced the attention mechanism, later refined by Luong et al. (2015). It is essentially a heat map of the token correlations in both sentences. Higher values mean more correlated words. To compute a value a_{ij} in the attention matrix a, we first score the influence of each hidden state on the word j. We then normalize each hidden state vector i by its normalized score and sum all of them up. By making this matrix a parameter of the model, the scoring is learned along with the other parameters of the network.

Attention works very well for word alignment of input and output in machine translation (see Figure 27), but it is also useful for classification, as it captures complex expressions. When attention is applied to the input and a copy of itself, it captures long-term syntactic and semantic relations between words (see example in Figure 26). Adding this **self-attention** to CNNs made them better at classification without increasing the parameter space too much.

14.4 The Transformer

For a while, it was unclear which architecture was better for text analysis, CNNs or RNNs. Much of the discussion focused on contextuality and long-range dependencies. Attention resolved this question, albeit by replacing both architectures with a third one: the **transformer**.

Vaswani et al. (2017) introduced the transformer model, which combined the best of both worlds: the selective long range-dependency of LSTMs and the aggregate context of CNNs. As a result, transformer-based architectures have

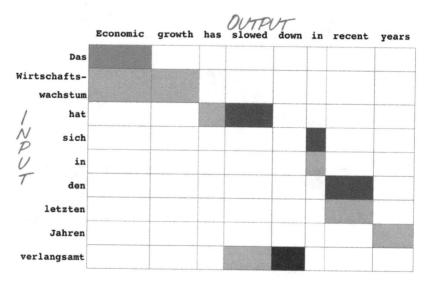

OUTPUT

INPUT

Figure 27 Attention in an RNN

dominated the leaderboards of various NLP tasks since. The architecture of the transformer is like a series of Russian nesting dolls: two parts with six elements each, where each of the first six has two parts (one of which is replicated eight times), and each of the second six has three elements.[11]

At the highest level, the transformer consists of two components: an **encoder** and a **decoder** (see Figure 28). Both of them are made up of stacks of six smaller elements, which sequentially process the input sentence.[12]

Each of the encoder stack elements has two parts: a self-attention over the input and a simple feed-forward neural network into which the input is fed. Self-attention is simply the correlation of all input words with all other input words, and it is where most of the magic of the transformer happens. We first create three hidden state "views" of the input, called the **query, key, and value** (each view is derived from the input via a dedicated weight set). We combine the key and query vectors and compute the probability distribution over the normalized sums, then multiply the result by the value vector (see Figure 29).

This process is repeated eight times in each layer,[13] once by each **attention head**. This has a similar effect as running several filters of the same region

---

[11] For an animated step-by-step visualization of the transformer, see http://jalammar .github.io/illustrated-transformer/.
[12] The number six is arbitrary and can be changed.
[13] Again, this number is an arbitrary choice.

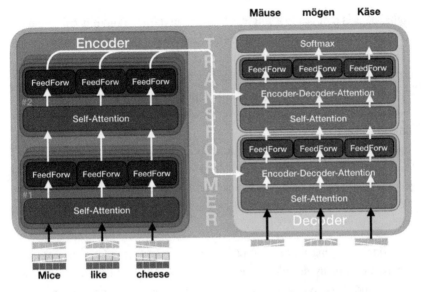

Figure 28 A schematic of the transformer

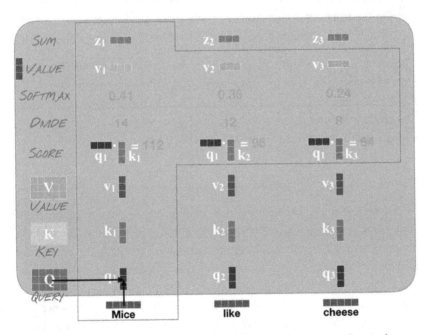

Figure 29 A simplified schematic of the transformer encoder stack

size in CNNs. Each attention head learns to attend to a different aspect of the data. For example, one might capture coreference relations between pronouns and their referents. Another might capture verbal relations. The output of the eight heads is reduced to a single self-attention result before it is fed through a feed-forward neural network, which produces an output for each word.

Self-attention and the multiple heads capture a lot of local contexts, but they are still local: They lose where a word came from in the sentence. In order to encode this positional component, the input embeddings are multiplied by a **positional encoding**. One of the ways in which this can be done is with a long sinusoidal wave.

The combination of self-attention with eight heads plus network is one of the six encoding elements. These elements are stacked, with each element receiving the output of the previous one. For the output of the last encoder, we again compute a key and a value vector to produce an overall encoding representation.

This final encoding representation is passed on to each of the six decoders. (There are as many decoders as encoders.) In addition to the encoding input, each decoder receives the output of the previous decoding element. Each decoder again has several components: a self-attention layer, attention over the encoder element (with which it is later combined), and a feed-forward network. The final decoder output is passed through a softmax layer for prediction.

The cost of the model is its complexity: In order to train the numerous parameters of a transformer, we need sufficient data and computing power. While the former is becoming less of an issue, the latter has attracted some attention. The machines necessary for training consume a substantial amount of energy, which impacts the environment (Strubell et al., 2019).

14.5 Neural Language Models

Neural networks also changed the field of language models, a class of **self-supervised** models in which each word serves as the input and as the output of the previous word. Traditionally, these models used probabilistic frameworks to compute the likelihood of a sequence of words. For computational feasibility, this involved computing the probability of each word in the limited context of the previous n words: we would break the probability of a sentence down into the product of the conditional probabilities of a word given its limited history of n previous words, $P(w_i|w_{i-n}, \ldots, w_{i-1})$.

Recurrent neural networks expanded this history limitation to include potentially unlimited prior context. As a result, language models got a lot better. The transformer also made a mark on this field. Using its best-of-both-worlds capabilities, a language model based on the transformer captures both long-range dependencies and local coherence. The most famous transformer-based

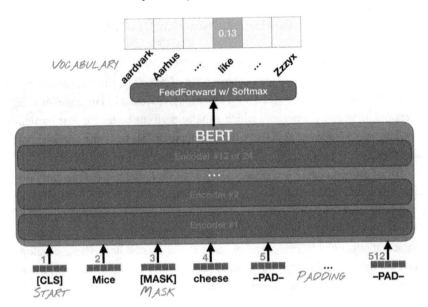

Figure 30 A schematic of BERT

language model is Generative Pretrained Transformer (**GPT**) (Radford et al., 2018). It was so convincing in producing realistic-looking text that the inventors did not release the full model initially, for fear of abuse. They eventually released a scaled-down version in GPT2 (Radford et al., 2019) and a companion piece discussing the implications (Solaiman et al., 2019).

Another transformer-based language model is BERT (Devlin et al., 2019). BERT officially stands for *bidirectional encoder representations from transformers*, following an unexplained trend to name embedding models after Sesame Street characters. It uses the transformer, but in both directions, to perform a cloze task (i.e., fill the blank). It takes a sentence in context and learns a representation encoding of it while learning to predict randomly blanked out words (i.e., they are replaced with a MASK token). At the beginning of each sentence, BERT uses a special classification token (CLS), which represents the entire sentence and is often used as input for classifiers. See Figure 30 for an example.

These representations have proven so adept at capturing semantic and syntactic information that they have improved almost any task where they were used. This includes both NLP tasks and social science applications: Vicinanza et al. (2020) used a BERT-based measure of prescience to predict which ideas would become influential in a field. BERT's success has been so complete that a cottage industry of papers dissecting BERT and its capabilities has emerged.

Some people are now speaking (only half-jokingly) of BERTology (Rogers et al., 2020).

The original paper included a multilingual version, which allows training a model on one language where we have a lot of data (say, English) and applying it to another language (**zero-shot learning**). A wealth of language-specific versions have since emerged, which usually perform better for that particular language (Nozza et al., 2020), but of course do not facilitate cross-lingual learning.

All of these models have emerged in a very short amount of time, but have steadily increased in capabilities and performance. It is not clear what we will see in the next few years, but it is clear that we have not yet reached the end of what they can do. There are still tasks to be solved, and we are only now starting to see applications to new areas of language understanding. These developments might upend everything written here, or they might build on it. Either way, I hope this Element has enabled you to tackle them in stride!

References

Adamson, A. S., & Smith, A. (2018). Machine learning and health care disparities in dermatology. *JAMA Dermatology, 154*(11), 1247–1248.

Alowibdi, J. S., Buy, U. A., & Yu, P. (2013). Empirical evaluation of profile characteristics for gender classification on Twitter. In *12th International Conference on Machine Learning and Applications (Volume 1)* (pp. 365–369).

Angwin, J., Larson, J., Mattu, S., & Kirchner, L. (2016). Machine bias. *ProPublica, May, 23.*

Atalay, S., El Kihal, S., & Ellsaesser, F. (2019). A natural language processing approach to predicting the persuasiveness of marketing communications. *SSRN 3410351.*

Bahdanau, D., Cho, K., & Bengio, Y. (2014). Neural machine translation by jointly learning to align and translate. *arXiv preprint arXiv:1409.0473.*

Bahdanau, D., Cho, K., & Bengio, Y. (2015). Neural machine translation by jointly learning to align and translate. In *3rd International Conference on Learning Representations.*

Bamman, D., O'Connor, B., & Smith, N. (2012). Censorship and deletion practices in Chinese social media. *First Monday, 17*(3).

Bender, E. M., & Friedman, B. (2018). Data statements for natural language processing: Toward mitigating system bias and enabling better science. *Transactions of the Association for Computational Linguistics, 6,* 587–604. https://doi.org/10.1162/tacl_a_00041

Berg-Kirkpatrick, T., Burkett, D., & Klein, D. (2012). An empirical investigation of statistical significance in NLP. In *Proceedings of the 2012 Joint Conference on Empirical Methods in Natural Language Processing and Computational Natural Language Learning* (pp. 995–1005).

Bhatia, S. (2017). Associative judgment and vector space semantics. *Psychological Review, 124*(1), 1.

Bolukbasi, T., Chang, K.-W., Zou, J. Y., Saligrama, V., & Kalai, A. T. (2016). Man is to computer programmer as woman is to homemaker? Debiasing word embeddings. In *30th Conference on Neural Information Processing Systems (NIPS 2016)*, Barcelona, Spain (pp. 4349–4357).

Chatsiou, K., & Mikhaylov, S. J. (2020). Deep learning for political science. *arXiv preprint arXiv:2005.06540.*

Chollet, F. (2017). *Deep learning with Python.* Manning.

Ciot, M., Sonderegger, M., & Ruths, D. (2013). Gender inference of Twitter users in non-english contexts. In *Proceedings of the 2013 Conference on Empirical Methods in Natural Language Processing* (pp. 18–21).

Coavoux, M., Narayan, S., & Cohen, S. B. (2018). Privacy-preserving neural representations of text. In *Proceedings of the 2018 Conference on Empirical Methods in Natural Language Processing* (pp. 1–10).

Collins, M. (2002). Discriminative training methods for hidden Markov models: Theory and experiments with perceptron algorithms. In *Proceedings of the 2002 Conference on Empirical Methods in Natural Language Processing* (pp. 1–8). Association for Computational Linguistics. www.aclweb.org/anthology/W02-1001. http://doi.org/10.3115/1118693.1118694.

Coussement, K., & Van den Poel, D. (2008). Churn prediction in subscription services: An application of support vector machines while comparing two parameter-selection techniques. *Expert Systems with Applications, 34*(1), 313–327.

De Choudhury, M., Counts, S., & Horvitz, E. J. (2013). Predicting postpartum changes in emotion and behavior via social media. In *Proceedings of the Sigchi Conference on Human Factors in Computing Systems* (pp. 3267–3276).

De Choudhury, M., Counts, S., Horvitz, E. J., & Hoff, A. (2014). Characterizing and predicting postpartum depression from shared facebook data. In *Proceedings of the 17th ACM Conference on Computer Supported Cooperative Work & Social Computing* (pp. 626–638).

Dell, G. S. (1986). A spreading-activation theory of retrieval in sentence production. *Psychological Review, 93*(3), 283.

Devlin, J., Chang, M.-W., Lee, K., & Toutanova, K. (2019). BERT: Pre-training of deep bidirectional transformers for language understanding. In *Proceedings of the 2019 Conference of the North American Chapter of the Association for Computational Linguistics: Human Language Technologies (Volume 1: Long and Short Papers)* (pp. 4171–4186).

Elazar, Y., & Goldberg, Y. (2018). Adversarial removal of demographic attributes from text data. In *Proceedings of the 2018 Conference on Empirical Methods in Natural Language Processing* (pp. 11–21).

Eliashberg, J., Hui, S. K., & Zhang, Z. J. (2007). From story line to box office: A new approach for green-lighting movie scripts. *Management Science, 53*(6), 881–893.

Evans, M., McIntosh, W., Lin, J., & Cates, C. (2007). Recounting the courts? Applying automated content analysis to enhance empirical legal research. *Journal of Empirical Legal Studies, 4*(4), 1007–1039.

Fort, K., Adda, G., & Cohen, K. B. (2011). Last words: Amazon Mechanical Turk: Gold mine or coal mine? *Computational Linguistics, 37*(2), 413–420. www.aclweb.org/anthology/J11-2010. http://doi.org/10.1162/COLI_a_00057.

Garg, N., Schiebinger, L., Jurafsky, D., & Zou, J. (2018). Word embeddings quantify 100 years of gender and ethnic stereotypes. *Proceedings of the National Academy of Sciences, 115*(16), E3635–E3644.

Gerber, M. S. (2014). Predicting crime using twitter and kernel density estimation. *Decision Support Systems, 61*, 115–125.

Goldberg, Y. (2016). A primer on neural network models for natural language processing. *Journal of Artificial Intelligence Research, 57*, 345–420.

Goldberg, Y. (2017). Neural network methods for natural language processing. *Synthesis Lectures on Human Language Technologies, 10*(1), 1–309.

Goldstein, D. G., & Gigerenzer, G. (2002). Models of ecological rationality: The recognition heuristic. *Psychological Review, 109*(1), 75.

Gonen, H., & Goldberg, Y. (2019, June). Lipstick on a pig: Debiasing methods cover up systematic gender biases in word embeddings but do not remove them. In *Proceedings of the 2019 Conference of the North American Chapter of the Association for Computational Linguistics: Human Language Technologies (Volume 1: Long and Short Papers)* (pp. 609–614). www.aclweb.org/anthology/N19-1061. http://doi.org/10.18653/v1/N19-1061.

Greene, K. T., Park, B., & Colaresi, M. (2019). Machine learning human rights and wrongs: How the successes and failures of supervised learning algorithms can inform the debate about information effects. *Political Analysis, 27*(2), 223–230.

Harwell, D. (2018). The accent gap. Why some accents don't work on Alexa or Google Home. *The Washington Post.* www.washingtonpost.com/graphics/2018/business/alexa-does-not-understand-your-accent/.

Henrich, J., Heine, S. J., & Norenzayan, A. (2010). The weirdest people in the world? *Behavioral and Brain Sciences, 33*(2–3), 61–83.

Hinton, G. E., Srivastava, N., Krizhevsky, A., Sutskever, I., & Salakhutdinov, R. R. (2012). Improving neural networks by preventing co-adaptation of feature detectors. In *30th Conference on Neural Information Processing Systems (NIPS 2016)*, Barcelona, Spain

Hochreiter, S., & Schmidhuber, J. (1997). Long short-term memory. *Neural Computation*, *9*(8), 1735–1780.

Hofman, J. M., Sharma, A., & Watts, D. J. (2017). Prediction and explanation in social systems. *Science*, *355*(6324), 486–488.

Hovy, D. (2016). The enemy in your own camp: How well can we detect statistically-generated fake reviews – An adversarial study. In *Proceedings of the 54th Annual Meeting of the Association for Computational Linguistics*. Association for Computational Linguistics. (pp. 351–356). http://doi.org/10.18653/v1/P16-2057

Hovy, D. (2020). *Text analysis in Python for social scientists: Discovery and exploration.* Cambridge University Press.

Hovy, D., Berg-Kirkpatrick, T., Vaswani, A., & Hovy, E. (2013). Learning whom to trust with MACE. In *Proceedings of the 2013 Conference of the North American Chapter of the Association for Computational Linguistics: Human Language Technologies* (pp. 1120–1130).

Hovy, D., & Søgaard, A. (2015). Tagging performance correlates with author age. In *Proceedings of the 53rd Annual Meeting of the Association for Computational Linguistics and the 7th International Joint Conference on Natural Language Processing (Volume 2: Short Papers)* (pp. 483–488).

Hovy, D., & Spruit, S. L. (2016). The social impact of natural language processing. In *Proceedings of the 54th Annual Meeting of the Association for Computational Linguistics (Volume 2: Short Papers)* (pp. 591–598).

Huang, H., Wen, Z., Yu, D., Ji, H., Sun, Y., Han, J., & Li, H. (2013). Resolving entity morphs in censored data. In *Proceedings of the 51st Annual Meeting of the Association for Computational Linguistics (Volume 1: Long Papers)* (pp. 1083–1093).

Humphreys, A., & Wang, R. J.-H. (2017). Automated text analysis for consumer research. *Journal of Consumer Research*, *44*(6), 1274–1306.

Jonas, H. (1984). *The imperative of responsibility: Foundations of an ethics for the technological age* (Original in German: Prinzip Verantwortung). University of Chicago Press.

Jørgensen, A., Hovy, D., & Søgaard, A. (2015). Challenges of studying and processing dialects in social media. In *Proceedings of the Workshop on Noisy User-Generated Text* (pp. 9–18).

Joshi, P., Santy, S., Budhiraja, A., Bali, K., & Choudhury, M. (2020, July). The state and fate of linguistic diversity and inclusion in the NLP world. In *Proceedings of the 58th Annual Meeting of the Association for Computational Linguistics* (pp. 6282–6293). Association for Computational Linguistics. www.aclweb.org/anthology/2020.acl-main.560. http://doi.org/10.18653/v1/2020.acl-main.560.

Kiritchenko, S., & Mohammad, S. (2018). Examining gender and race bias in two hundred sentiment analysis systems. In *Proceedings of the Seventh Joint Conference on Lexical and Computational Semantics* (pp. 43–53).

Konečný, J., McMahan, H. B., Yu, F. X., Richtárik, P., Suresh, A. T., & Bacon, D. (2016). Federated learning: Strategies for improving communication efficiency. *arXiv preprint arXiv:1610.05492.*

Kozlowski, A. C., Taddy, M., & Evans, J. A. (2018). The geometry of culture: Analyzing meaning through word embeddings. *arXiv preprint arXiv:1803.09288.*

Kurita, K., Vyas, N., Pareek, A., Black, A. W., & Tsvetkov, Y. (2019, August). Measuring bias in contextualized word representations. In *Proceedings of the First Workshop on Gender Bias in Natural Language Processing* (pp. 166–172). Association for Computational Linguistics. www.aclweb.org/anthology/W19-3823. http://doi.org/10.18653/v1/W19-3823.

Le, Q., & Mikolov, T. (2014). Distributed representations of sentences and documents. In *Proceedings of the 31st International Conference on Machine Learning* (pp. 1188–1196).

Levelt, W. J. (1993). *Speaking: From intention to articulation* (Vol. 1). MIT Press.

Lewis-Kraus, G. (2016). The great AI awakening. *The New York Times, 14.* www.nytimes.com/2016/12/14/magazine/the-great-ai-awakening.html.

Li, Y., Baldwin, T., & Cohn, T. (2018). Towards robust and privacy-Preserving text representations. In *Proceedings of the 56th Annual Meeting of the Association for Computational Linguistics (Volume 2: Short Papers)* (pp. 25–30).

Liu, W., & Ruths, D. (2013). What's in a name? Using first names as features for gender inference in Twitter. In *Analyzing Microtext: 2013 AAAI Spring Symposium (10–16).*

Lucy, L., Demszky, D., Bromley, P., & Jurafsky, D. (2020). Content analysis of textbooks via natural language processing: Findings on gender, race, and ethnicity in Texas U.S. history textbooks. *AERA Open, 6*(3), 2332858420940312.

Luong, T., Pham, H., & Manning, C.D. (2015, September). Effective approaches to attention-based neural machine translation. In *Proceedings of the 2015 Conference on Empirical Methods in Natural Language Processing* (pp. 1412–1421). Association for Computational Linguistics. www.aclweb.org/anthology/D15-1166. http://doi.org/10.18653/v1/D15-1166.

Manning, C. D. (2015). Computational linguistics and deep learning. *Computational Linguistics*, *41*(4), 701–707.

Marsland, S. (2011). *Machine learning: An algorithmic perspective.* Chapman and Hall/CRC.

Meinshausen, N., & Bühlmann, P. (2010). Stability selection. *Journal of the Royal Statistical Society: Series B (Statistical Methodology)*, *72*(4), 417–473.

Mikolov, T., Sutskever, I., Chen, K., Corrado, G. S., & Dean, J. (2013). Distributed representations of words and phrases and their compositionality. In *30th Conference on Neural Information Processing Systems (NIPS 2016)*, Barcelona, Spain (pp. 3111–3119).

Mills, S. (2012). *Gender matters: Feminist linguistic analysis.* Equinox.

Minsky, M., & Papert, S. A. (1969). *Perceptrons.* MIT Press.

Mohammady, E., & Culotta, A. (2014). Using county demographics to infer attributes of Twitter users. In *Proceedings of the Joint Workshop on Social Dynamics and Personal Attributes in Social Media* (pp. 7–16).

Mohri, M., Rostamizadeh, A., & Talwalkar, A. (2018). *Foundations of machine learning.* MIT Press.

Mosteller, F., & Wallace, D. L. (1963). Inference in an authorship problem: A comparative study of discrimination methods applied to the authorship of the disputed Federalist Papers. *Journal of the American Statistical Association*, *58*(302), 275–309.

Munro, R. (2013). NLP for all languages. *Idibon Blog, May 22. http://idibon .com/nlp-for-all.*

Nguyen, D., Smith, N. A., & Rosé, C. P. (2011). Author age prediction from text using linear regression. In *Proceedings of the 5th ACL-HLT Workshop on Language Technology for Cultural Heritage, Social Sciences, and Humanities* (pp. 115–123).

Niculae, V., Kumar, S., Boyd-Graber, J., & Danescu-Niculescu-Mizil, C. (2015). Linguistic harbingers of betrayal: A case study on an online strategy game. In *Proceedings of the 53rd Annual Meeting of the Association for Computational Linguistics and the 7th International Joint Conference on Natural Language Processing (Volume 1: Long Papers)* (pp. 1650–1659).

Nozza, D., Bianchi, F., & Hovy, D. (2020). What the [MASK]? Making sense of language-specific BERT models. *arXiv preprint arXiv:2003.02912.*

O'Neil, C. (2016). The ethical data scientist. *Slate, February 4. www.slate .com/articles/technology/future_tense/2016/02/how_to_bring_better_ ethics_to_data_science.html.*

Park, B., Colaresi, M., & Greene, K. (2018). Beyond a bag of words: Using pulsar to extract judgments on specific human rights at scale. *Peace Economics, Peace Science and Public Policy, 24*(4).

Park, G., Schwartz, H. A., Eichstaedt, J. C., Kern, M. L., Kosinski, M., Stillwell, D. J., ... Seligman, M. E. (2015). Automatic personality assessment through social media language. *Journal of Personality and Social Psychology, 108*(6), 934.

Passonneau, R. J., & Carpenter, B. (2014). The benefits of a model of annotation. *Transactions of the Association for Computational Linguistics, 2*, 311–326. www.aclweb.org/anthology/Q14-1025. http://doi.org/10.1162/tacl_a_00185.

Paun, S., Carpenter, B., Chamberlain, J., Hovy, D., Kruschwitz, U., & Poesio, M. (2018). Comparing Bayesian models of annotation. *Transactions of the Association for Computational Linguistics, 6*, 571–585. https://doi.org/10.1162/tacl_a_00040

Pavlick, E., Post, M., Irvine, A., Kachaev, D., & Callison-Burch, C. (2014). The language demographics of Amazon Mechanical Turk. *Transactions of the Association for Computational Linguistics, 2*, 79–92. www.aclweb.org/anthology/Q14-1007. http://doi.org/10.1162/tacl_a_00167.

Peskov, D., Cheng, B., Elgohary, A., Barrow, J., Danescu-Niculescu-Mizil, C., & Boyd-Graber, J. (2020, July). It takes two to lie: One to lie, and one to listen. In *Proceedings of the 58th Annual Meeting of the Association for Computational Linguistics* (pp. 3811–3854). Association for Computational Linguistics. www.aclweb.org/anthology/2020.acl-main.353.

Peterson, A., & Spirling, A. (2018). Classification accuracy as a substantive quantity of interest: Measuring polarization in westminster systems. *Political Analysis, 26*(1), 120–128.

Plank, B., Hovy, D., & Søgaard, A. (2014). Learning part-of-speech taggers with inter-annotator agreement loss. In *Proceedings of the 14th Conference of the European Chapter of the Association for Computational Linguistics* (pp. 742–751).

Pomerleau, D. A. (1989). Alvinn: An autonomous land vehicle in a neural network. In *Advances in Neural Information Processing Systems* (pp. 305–313).

Pomerleau, D. A. (2012). *Neural network perception for mobile robot guidance* (Vol. 239). Springer Science & Business Media.

Prabhakaran, V., Rambow, O., & Diab, M. (2012). Predicting overt display of power in written dialogs. In *Proceedings of the 2012 Conference of the North*

American Chapter of the Association for Computational Linguistics: Human Language Technologies (pp. 518–522).

Preoţiuc-Pietro, D., Lampos, V., & Aletras, N. (2015a). An analysis of the user occupational class through Twitter content. In *Proceedings of the 53rd Annual Meeting of the Association for Computational Linguistics and the 7th International Joint Conference on Natural Language Processing (Volume 1: Long Papers)* (pp. 1754–1764)

Preoţiuc-Pietro, D., Volkova, S., Lampos, V., Bachrach, Y., & Aletras, N. (2015b). Studying user income through language, behaviour and affect in social media. *PloS One*, 10(9), e0138717.

Radford, A., Narasimhan, K., Salimans, T., & Sutskever, I. (2018). Improving language understanding by generative pre-training. https://s3-us-west-2. amazonaws. com/openaiassets/researchcovers/languageunsupervised/language understanding paper.pdf.

Radford, A., Wu, J., Child, R., Luan, D., Amodei, D., & Sutskever, I. (2019). Language models are unsupervised multitask learners. *OpenAI Blog, 1*(8), 9.

Rogaway, P. (2015). *The moral character of cryptographic work* (Technical Report). IACR-Cryptology ePrint Archive.

Rogers, A., Kovaleva, O., & Rumshisky, A. (2020). A primer in BERTology: What we know about how BERT works. *arXiv preprint arXiv:2002.12327.*

Rosenblatt, F. (1958). The perceptron: A probabilistic model for information storage and organization in the brain. *Psychological Review, 65*(6), 386.

Rosenthal, S., & McKeown, K. (2011). Age prediction in blogs: A study of style, content, and online behavior in pre-and post-social media generations. In *Proceedings of the 49th Annual Meeting of the Association for Computational Linguistics: Human Language Technologies (Volume 1)* (pp. 763–772).

Rudinger, R., Naradowsky, J., Leonard, B., & Van Durme, B. (2018). Gender bias in coreference resolution. In *Proceedings of the 2018 Conference of the North American Chapter of the Association for Computational Linguistics: Human Language Technologies (Volume 2: Short Papers)* (pp. 8–14).

Sap, M., Card, D., Gabriel, S., Choi, Y., & Smith, N. A. (2019, July). The risk of racial bias in hate speech detection. In *Proceedings of the 57th Conference of the Association for Computational Linguistics* (pp. 1668–1678). Association for Computational Linguistics. www.aclweb.org/anthology/P19-1163.

Sap, M., Gabriel, S., Qin, L., Jurafsky, D., Smith, N. A., & Choi, Y. (2020, July). Social bias frames: Reasoning about social and power implications of language. In *Proceedings of the 58th Annual Meeting of the Association for Computational Linguistics* (pp. 5477–5490). Association for Computational Linguistics. www.aclweb.org/anthology/2020.acl-main.486.

Schnoebelen, T. (2013). The weirdest languages. *Idibon Blog, June 21.* *http://idibon.com/the-weirdest-languages.*

Shah, D. S., Schwartz, H. A., & Hovy, D. (2020, July). Predictive biases in natural language processing models: A conceptual framework and overview. In *Proceedings of the 58th Annual Meeting of the Association for Computational Linguistics* (pp. 5248–5264). Association for Computational Linguistics. www.aclweb.org/anthology/2020.acl-main.468. http://doi.org/10.18653/v1/2020.acl-main.468.

Shmueli, G. (2010). To explain or to predict? *Statistical Science, 25*(3), 289–310.

Snow, R., O'Connor, B., Jurafsky, D., & Ng, A. (2008, October). Cheap and fast – but is it good? Evaluating non-expert annotations for natural language tasks. In *Proceedings of the 2008 Conference on Empirical Methods in Natural Language Processing* (pp. 254–263). Association for Computational Linguistics. www.aclweb.org/anthology/D08-1027.

Solaiman, I., Brundage, M., Clark, J., Askell, A., Herbert-Voss, A., Wu, J., ... Wang, J. (2019). Release strategies and the social impacts of language models. *arXiv preprint arXiv:1908.09203.*

Spärck Jones, K. (1972). A statistical interpretation of term specificity and its application in retrieval. *Journal of Documentation, 28*(1), 11–21.

Strubell, E., Ganesh, A., & McCallum, A. (2019, July). Energy and policy considerations for deep learning in NLP. In *Proceedings of the 57th Annual Meeting of the Association for Computational Linguistics* (pp. 3645–3650). Association for Computational Linguistics. www.aclweb.org/anthology/P19-1355. http://doi.org/10.18653/v1/P19-1355.

Sunstein, C. R. (2004). Precautions against what? The availability heuristic and cross-cultural risk perceptions. *University of Chicago John M. Olin Law & Economics Working Paper*, No. 220, 4–22.

Tan, Y. C., & Celis, L. E. (2019). Assessing social and intersectional biases in contextualized word representations. In *30th Conference on Neural Information Processing Systems (NIPS 2016)*, Barcelona, Spain (pp. 13230–13241).

Tatman, R. (2017). Gender and dialect bias in YouTube's automatic captions. In *Proceedings of the First ACL Workshop on Ethics in Natural Language Processing* (pp. 53–59).

Tetreault, J., Burstein, J., & Leacock, C. (2015). Proceedings of the Tenth Workshop on Innovative Use of NLP for Building Educational Applications. *Association for Computational Linguistics.* http://aclweb.org/anthology/W15-0600

Tirunillai, S., & Tellis, G. J. (2012). Does chatter really matter? Dynamics of user-generated content and stock performance. *Marketing Science, 31*(2), 198–215.

Tversky, A., & Kahneman, D. (1973). Availability: A heuristic for judging frequency and probability. *Cognitive Psychology, 5*(2), 207–232.

Vaswani, A., Shazeer, N., Parmar, N., Uszkoreit, J., Jones, L., Gomez, A. N., ... Polosukhin, I. (2017). Attention is all you need. In *30th Conference on Neural Information Processing Systems (NIPS 2016)*, Barcelona, Spain (pp. 5998–6008).

Vicinanza, P., Goldberg, A., & Srivastava, S. (2020). Who sees the future? A deep learning language model demonstrates the vision advantage of being small. https://doi.org/10.31235/osf.io/j24pw

Volkova, S., Bachrach, Y., Armstrong, M., & Sharma, V. (2015, January). Inferring latent user properties from texts published in social media (demo). In *Proceedings of the Twenty-Ninth Conference on Artificial Intelligence* (pp. 4296–4297).

Volkova, S., Coppersmith, G., & Van Durme, B. (2014). Inferring user political preferences from streaming communications. In *Proceedings of the 52nd Annual Meeting of the Association for Computational Linguistics* (pp. 186–196).

Wu, Y., Schuster, M., Chen, Z., Le, Q. V., Norouzi, M., Macherey, W., & Dean, J. (2016). Google's neural machine translation system: Bridging the gap between human and machine translation. *arXiv preprint arXiv: 1609.08144.*

Yarkoni, T., & Westfall, J. (2017). Choosing prediction over explanation in psychology: Lessons from machine learning. *Perspectives on Psychological Science, 12*(6), 1100–1122.

Yatskar, M., Zettlemoyer, L., & Farhadi, A. (2016). Situation recognition: Visual semantic role labeling for image understanding. In *Proceedings of the IEEE Conference on Computer Vision and Pattern Recognition* (pp. 5534–5542).

Zhao, J., Wang, T., Yatskar, M., Ordonez, V., & Chang, K.-W. (2017). Men also like shopping: Reducing gender bias amplification using corpus-level constraints. In *Proceedings of the 2017 Conference on Empirical Methods in Natural Language Processing* (pp. 2979–2989).

Acknowledgements

Thanks again to Mike Alvarez and Neal Beck for sticking with me and encouraging this Element, to Robert Dreesen and the CUP staff for shepherding it, and you, for reading it. Thanks are due to the students of my classes testing out the material and finding flaws and mistakes, and to the people who got in touch after the first Element with kind words and feedback.

I dedicate this work, with love, to Nel and Leo.

Cambridge Elements ≡

Quantitative and Computational Methods for the Social Sciences

R. Michael Alvarez
California Institute of Technology

R. Michael Alvarez has taught at the California Institute of Technology his entire career, focusing on elections, voting behavior, election technology, and research methodologies. He has written or edited a number of books (recently, *Computational Social Science: Discovery and Prediction*, and *Evaluating Elections: A Handbook of Methods and Standards*) and numerous academic articles and reports.

Nathaniel Beck
New York University

Nathaniel Beck is Professor of Politics at NYU (and Affiliated Faculty at the NYU Center for Data Science) where he has been since 2003, before which he was Professor of Political Science at the University of California, San Diego. He is the founding editor of the quarterly, *Political Analysis*. He is a fellow of both the American Academy of Arts and Sciences and the Society for Political Methodology.

About the Series

The Elements Series Quantitative and Computational Methods for the Social Sciences contains short introductions and hands-on tutorials to innovative methodologies. These are often so new that they have no textbook treatment or no detailed treatment on how the method is used in practice. Among emerging areas of interest for social scientists, the series presents machine learning methods, the use of new technologies for the collection of data and new techniques for assessing causality with experimental and quasi-experimental data.

Cambridge Elements ☰

Quantitative and Computational Methods for the Social Sciences

Elements in the Series

Twitter as Data
Zachary C. Steinert-Threlkeld

A Practical Introduction to Regression Discontinuity Designs: Foundations
Matias D. Cattaneo, Nicolás Idrobo and Rocío Titiunik

Agent-Based Models of Social Life: Fundamentals
Michael Laver

Agent-Based Models of Polarization and Ethnocentrism
Michael Laver

Images as Data for Social Science Research: An Introduction to Convolutional Neural Nets for Image Classification
Nora Webb Williams, Andreu Casas and John D. Wilkerson

Target Estimation and Adjustment Weighting for Survey Nonresponse and Sampling Bias
Devin Caughey, Adam J. Berinsky, Sara Chatfield, Erin Hartman, Eric Schickler and Jasjeet S. Sekhon

Text Analysis in Python for Social Scientists: Discovery and Exploration
Dirk Hovy

Unsupervised Machine Learning for Clustering in Political and Social Research
Philip D. Waggoner

Using Shiny to Teach Econometric Models
Shawna K. Metzger

Modern Dimension Reduction
Philip D. Waggoner

Text Analysis in Python for Social Scientists: Prediction and Classification
Dirk Hovy

A full series listing is available at: www.cambridge.org/QCMSS

Printed in the USA
CPSIA information can be obtained
at www.ICGtesting.com
LVHW010003211223
767096LV00013B/592

9 781108 958508